By the same aut

Novels

Only the Wind is Free
A Measure of Peace
A Fragment of Time
The Future is Ours
Canopy of Silence
Annie's Promise
Look Within Your Heart
A Distant Dream
A Bitter Legacy
Out of the Night
Practising Wearing Purple
A Bed of Roses

__Writing Awake the Dreamweaver__ A motivational handbook designed to release creativity

Margaret has written two plays, co-researched a television documentary which grew out of Canopy of Silence. She has written many short stories and features.

She has judged writing competitions and taught creative writing internationally for many years through her own workshops and those of others such as Arvon. She also mentors students. She believes that creative writing is good for the soul, and is within the reach of everyone.

She is Writer in Residence at Yeovil Arts Centre, Co-administrator of the Yeovil Community Arts Association Literary Section, co-founder of the fundraising International Yeovil Literary Prize, and leader of the team of judges.

Examples of Praise for Margaret

Writing Awake the Dreamweaver
'The magic of Margaret… inspirational' Rachel Cuperman, Film Producer, writer and former a student of Margaret's

'Wise and inspiring.' Nikki Gemmell, acclaimed international author

Practising Wearing Purple

'First-class… a delightful novel, full of sympathy, understanding and drama…' Tim Manderson, Publishing News

Only the Wind is Free

'Vivid, sensuous, warm-hearted, this novel marks a most impressive literary debut' Barry Unsworth, Booker Prize winner

Canopy of Silence

'Superior and moving writing marks out this memorable story'.
Daily Mail

Writing Workshops

'She gave me confidence in my abilities.' Louise Harding, winner of a writing prize.

'It's not just her teaching; she cares.' James Mitchell. Published Author.

'Her workshops are not only enhancing, but such good fun.' Sylvia Fortnum

'Margaret is a generous writing mentor, combining encouragement and inspiration with honest critique. It is a pleasure to be writing under her guidance.' Raquelle Azran, published writer.

The Writer's Springboard

An exploration of the essentials of fiction writing

Margaret Graham

[signature: Margaret Graham]

Wordforce Publications

First published in 2006 by Wordforce Publications,
3 Barrowfield, Burton Bradstock, Bridport
Dorset DT6 4RH
www.thewordforce.com
www.margaret-graham.com

ISBN 0-9543724-1-7

A CIP catalogue record for this book is available from the British Library.

Printed and bound in the United Kingdom by
Creeds Printers, Broadoak, Bridport, Dorset

Wordforce Publications

For Megan and Josie, and all that join us later, and for Ros, Jim,
Tracy and Rachel
With love

Contents

INTRODUCTION – including SHOW and TELL

I often think that trying to understand the essentials of fiction writing can be compared to driving lessons. There you are, sitting with your belt on, being told to hold the wheel, look in the mirror, signal, depress the clutch, put it into gear, just a touch on the accelerator, look in the mirror again, and pull away. *'Yer what? How can I possibly drive the thing along a road, on top of thinking of all these bits and bobs.'*

We do though, don't we, and sooner than we think.

So it is with writing. My task in ***The Writer's Springboard*** is pretty much encompassed in the title. I am going to help you towards an understanding that will springboard you towards original, clear and empathetic creative writing. Towards creative writing skills that will satisfy you as the author, and involve the reader.

Using my course material honed over many years, with invaluable input from students, we are going to explore the essentials of fiction writing. In other words the structural form: plot, characters, motivation, theme, the use of flashbacks, tension/conflict and exposition (and the difference between TELL and SHOW exposition). We will work at developing empathy in order to create scenes which show not tell through use of dialogue, setting, body language, the use of the senses and symbolism. We will look at 'voice'.

We will look at the fundamental differences between the short story and the novel. I will talk you through my own strangely named technique for taking the stress out of turning the germ of an idea into a full blown fictional work. I call this the Zigzag Path. I will also give tips on the subplot, how to analyse the work of others to further your understanding of fiction writing, and have included a few notes on that little varmint, the synopsis. Don't worry if something is elusive in the early stages of the handbook. It will be repeated in another context and understanding will come.

But first of all, let me just give you an example of SHOW not TELL, which is what so many editors ask for, but don't explain. Forgive the content, but it is work I produced with the help of some children during a workshop. It was great fun, so thanks to the 'Desert Dingoes', as the children called themselves.

These excerpts should ease open the door of your understanding. Just read straight through, don't try and memorise or worry about it. It will lodge in your unconscious and get you going. Just enjoy!

This is the précis of the story I gave the children

Martin, a 9 year old boy, is travelling with his friends in a mini bus across the desert. They are hot and longing to arrive at their summer camp after an early morning start. Martin leans out of the window, staring down into the ravine they are driving alongside when there is a loud bang, and the bus careers out of control, towards the ravine. Only Martin escapes the plunge into the ravine. His teacher and classmates are trapped at the bottom of the ravine. His 'sort of' friend Henry is hurt. Mr Evans, his teacher calls up from the bus and tells Martin he must set off for the escarpment in the distance, and once there, climb it. From the top he should be able to see an airfield in the distance. He must head for this and get help. Their one mobile phone has been destroyed in the crash.

During his endeavours Martin not only overcomes all sorts of physical obstacles, but jeopardises himself to save others. In doing so he addresses and overcomes his selfishness born out of low self- esteem. He is left with a way forward, without sacrificing his own identity.

We produced this scene to illustrate TELL

TELL. (An excerpt)
*Martin was leaning out of the window in spite of another boy,Henry, nagging at him to come in. 'Come on Mart, sit down,' Henry said impatiently.(**The use of an adverb is <u>telling</u>. There should be a way to <u>show</u> through physical action, rhythm of language etc. Also, the writer has already told us Henry is nagging, and then gives us dialogue doing just that. It's best not to over-egg the pudding.**) Martin ignored him, because it was too hot inside the bus and he wanted the breeze. Henry then reminded him that Mr Evans would really penalise him this time, and probably the rest of the class too. Martin shrugged it off. He was nine not a toddler, and was quite old enough to make up his own mind. And why should he care if others got into trouble? That was just soft, and not the way to live your life, or so his brother always said. No, he wanted to stay*

standing and at the window, and watch the wide open spaces which were a million miles from the tenements of home.

The ravine was deep and the road skirted towards the edge and the wheels were kicking up the stones as Mr Evans tried to stay in the rut. But didn't the bus seem to be slipping out and then back in again? Martin felt scared suddenly at the nearness of the ravine, and wanted to sit down, but he could almost hear his brother calling him a wimp so he gripped the window frame tighter and continued to stare out. As he did so, there was a loud bang. For a moment Martin couldn't think what was happening, then the next thing he knew was that he was hanging onto the window frame for dear life as the bus careered out of control. Fearfully he felt himself falling and even Henry, who he felt grab his leg, couldn't quite stop him. Though for a moment he thought he had. He was terrified as he was thrown out of the window towards the road.

We are told that Martin is leaning out of the window, and we hear Henry urging him to sit down. Martin refuses because he wants to stand at the window, an action that ultimately brings about Martin's escape from the bus and his opportunity to set out for help. Though at the time it looks like disaster for him.

The kids and I needed to know why he was so defiant in order to understand his actions, and asked questions of ourselves and came up with an answer that suited us all; there was a brother and a troubled home life. We incorporated it into both the TELL and SHOW versions. In both, we included some interior monologue (thoughts) to indicate this situation, and hint that it was the root of his attitude problem.

We provided some tension in both versions, as you will see, and they were the same tensions. How did we create tension? By creating problems. For instance, Martin shouldn't be misbehaving. Will he or won't he be caught and all the class penalised? This is overtaken by the building crisis of the bus crash, bringing with it lots of tension because first the bus is in the rut again, and then is not. Then there is the bang of the tyre, and what did that mean? Then Martin is being flung out of the window and then perhaps he is saved. So, problem, solution, another problem, solution, and so on and so on. We 'held back' all along the way. How? A) We only hinted at the problems at home, we didn't go into detail. If Martin's interior monologue had given us the complete answer, the curiosity would be over.

B) We allowed the bus crash to b-u-i-l-d. The bus was in and out of the ruts. Then it didn't immediately go careering off into the ravine. It seemed Henry made an attempt to save him – almost but not quite.

In this TELL version we explained what was happening, and it all seems adequate.

Or is it? Can we do better, try harder, go that extra mile?

Let's see how we can SHOW this same scene. And that's the key - we're about to create a scene to SHOW what is happening in a way that invites maximum involvement as readers. We will 'stay in the moment' and expand and slow down the scene used in TELL. We will use empathy to get inside Martin, and draw on the senses such as sight, touch and sound. We will colour in the TELLING reportage of the previous excerpt. We will work really hard and use **all** our powers of exposition, our combined 'voice' to create a sense of place, a sense of anticipation, a sense of 'being there'. We will expand but not progress the plot. In other words, we will not move forward.

SHOW. (An excerpt)

'Mart, get back in.' Martin McDonald continued to lean out of the school mini-bus window ignoring Henry who was now pulling at his shorts. Who wouldn't want fresh air when it was like an oven inside? Now Martin felt Henry's moist breath on his leg, heard his whisper, louder this time. 'Mart, Evans'll really do you this time. Give yourself a break, and the rest of us. We'll all cop it if he sees you. You know he wants us all with seat belts on when he's driving.'

Martin slapped away Henry's hand. What a big girl's blouse. If it was a toss up between detention for everyone later, and the breeze for now, there was no choice was there? You had to take what you wanted in this life 'cos no-one will give it to you, that's what his brother always said. He gripped the frame tighter, snatching a look at Henry, who seemed fit to explode in the heat; his face was as red as his hair. Martin snapped, 'Leave me alone. You can damn well sit there, strapped in like a bawling baby, but it's hot, hot, hot, and I need air. If you're too much of a wimp, that's your look out.'

Martin turned back to the window, leaning further out this time, seeing the ground flashing past so quickly that the shrubs at the edge of the road were a blur. He shifted his gaze to the desert they were passing through, squinting against the dust. In the distance was an escarpment, way off to the east. Evans had said, 'The road goes the long way round, a long, long way round, to base camp which lies alongside a small airport.' He'd promised them all a flight to see the desert from the air, as a reward for patience on the journey. For a moment Martin hesitated, drawing back just a fraction. What if Evans saw him now? What if the flight went ahead without him?

He was jerked back towards the window, in time to see stones skim out from beneath the wheels. The bus zigzagged just a fraction, up and out of a rut, but then back into it. Evans must be trying to stay in the ruts which had scored deep into the hard baked track. Above the rush of the wind, Martin could hear the whine of the engine and now the track was running closer to the ravine. He relaxed. Old Evans had too much to do to check on what was happening behind him.

He felt Henry tugging again, and there was his breath on his leg - again. He wanted to wipe it away. It was as bad as sitting on a warmed up seat someone had just left. But then Martin shrugged, Henry might be a wimp, but he was the only one in school who seemed to want to be his friend. Maybe it was because he was different too. It can't be much fun being a carrot top with a gammy leg. This time he didn't slap his hand away, but turned slightly, his eyes watering from the dust and the wind. 'Come up with me, Henry. It'll cool you down.'

He saw Henry shake his head, and gesture down to Martin's seat, and the tangle of packed lunch and empty seat belt. 'Get back in.' he mouthed

Martin didn't bother to reply, and turned again to the desert. He loved the space, the blue sky, the fact that there were no ugly dirty tenements, no smell of blocked lavs, or rotting food. He breathed deeply, and moved up and down with the bucking bus. Was this what riding a horse was like?

He imagined how cowboys once rode across here, eyes and ears pricked for Indians. Well, good for the Indians, he'd fight if this was his land. Lucky the school won that bit of money on the lottery. Educational trips all round. He peered behind, but all he could see was the sand and dust billowing like a burst vacuum cleaner bag in the bus's wake. He weighed up the ravine they were still driving alongside. How wide was it? Maybe 20 metres? How deep? There was another lurch and they were in and out of the rut again, and the edge of the ravine was too near. Surely it was. Mart's grip tightened on the window frame as he stared down. Get back in the rut, he wanted to shout, and yes, Evans was slowing, and steering it back. Clunk. They were in it again.

Martin closed his eyes and really wanted to sit down now, but how could he, because then he'd hear his brother's voice in his head, calling him a wimp?

He half turned to Henry, but just as he did there was a loud bang. Henry looked up, Martin was thrown back, half out of the window. The sky was lurching, 'What,' he gasped, snatching at the frame, at anything, finding the upright as the bus skidded, and jerked up and out of the rut. Evans was braking, but the bus felt funny, and he could see the remains of the burst tyre flapping.

The bus started to spin. And spin. And spin. He was tossed to the left, banged his head on the upright, heard screaming in the bus, felt Henry clutch his shorts. Thank you, thank you.

But then it was as though he was being sucked out with every spin and jerk of the bus. Further and further, his arm was at full stretch as he clung to the upright, but his shoulders, his chest were hanging in space, being pushed by the wind, sucked by the spin. Out. Out.

Then, a touch on his leg, a hand, a hand that was gripping his thigh, holding, pulling him back. Henry's hand. Just an inch, and then another and the window dug into his hips, but it didn't matter. Another inch. The bus was still groaning and roaring over the screaming, but the ground was receding. It was. It was.

But then there was another jerk. The screaming was louder, and it was because it was from him, and he could taste the sand in his mouth and Henry's hand was slipping, Martin's arm was stretched, stretched, his fingers weakening on the upright, the ground closer. Then Henry's hand slipped again and was gone, and Martin was flying through the air and all around was splintering, screaming...

We'll just refer back to the TELL example in which you can see that the kids and I were explaining what was happening, much as we do if any of us witness an incident and then relate it to a friend. When a friend **tells** us something, we can't quite **see** and feel it, smell it, taste and hear it. We can't understand the nuances of actually being there. So we end up being less emotionally involved.

When we SHOWED the excerpt, a scene was created by quite literally 'staying in the moment' – we tried to 'be' Martin standing at the window of a moving bus. We tried to feel physically what he would feel, and work out how to use the setting and his actions to SHOW the real reason for this attitude.

For the SHOW excerpt we had to work out how we could incorporate the information, and SHOW it through action, dialogue and interior monologue, all without lengthy explanations and without progressing the plot beyond the point at which the TELLING example finished. We wanted the readers to feel as though they were there, so that they could be fully involved in Martin's role.

In the end we took three pages to SHOW our incorporated details of the past and present.

Let's look at the details of that incorporation.

We used the setting to show Martin's appreciation of the wide open spaces in comparison to his home environment, we used his brother's words to stop him sitting down and illustrated Martin's relationship with his brother. We were also able to show that Martin cared for his friend after all which gave us a different slant on Martin and his potential as a more pleasant person.

We set the scene and characters through the use of action, and the senses. We see hear and touch as Martin does. As in the TELL excerpt, we are in his point of view only, which means from inside himself but we used the senses to make it more powerful. Although Henry is there, and is second in importance in the scene, we never see the action from inside him. This is deliberate. To have been in both weakens the reader's identification with Martin, the main character.

By being in Martin's point of view we are invited to be complicit in this journey by being drawn inside him. Think of the story of Cinderella. If the action was seen from the point of view of, let's say a mouse in the larder, we wouldn't know how Cinders was feeling, really feeling. This is why it's important for you as the writer to think carefully about your characters. We need to learn to empathise, to *feel* ourselves in the setting, and more or less become the characters in each scene.

We'll talk more about this later.

We used tension as in the TELL example, but it was far more meaty in the SHOW. We were far more aware of Martin's emotion, of the details of – will he, won't he be seen by Evans? Of Henry's attempts to get him to sit down, of Henry's gammy leg, though the reason for this is 'held back' and is something else to be revealed later. We 'held back' during the tension build up to the bus crash; we were there inside Martin, feeling his reaction, and his rising panic, then his relief, but then panic again. And who of us hasn't felt this in some context or another. So it's easy to empathise, isn't it?

Let's look at the tension in the SHOW text again. There is the use of rhythm to show an increase in tension. What do I mean by this? We used shorter sentences as he comes out of the window because when we are frightened, we often think in gasps, much as our breathing alters. In other words, the style becomes staccato. If it had been a relaxed stage of the story, the language would have reflected this and flowed.

What else did we use in our SHOW excerpt?

Symbolism. One example is the way Martin slapped away Henry's hand, much like the slapping away of the rules. This is reinforced by his glance down at the empty seat belt. It symbolises his life, really. There's a certain emptiness to him, a lack of restraint. There's nothing clever in using symbolism, which is a loose tool these days. You'll do it, then sit back and think – how clever I am, there's a spot of symbolism. And you will have done it unconsciously. As writers we have to learn to trust our unconscious. It helps us all the way along if we let it. I'm sure you will find you are doing so, by the end of the book.

So, all together now, what is the key to SHOWING, to staying in the moment?

Empathy. The kids and I used empathy throughout. We eased into Martin's skin and into Henry's too, so that we understood in our own minds what each character would do in that situation, and how they would feel. My acting out of hanging onto an imagined upright, whilst a group made skidding noises and some poor child hung onto my leg was a sight to behold. Of course, everyone's interpretation was different, and had we each produced our own version of the précis we would have had a medley of stories, all as viable as the other. And that's the 'voice'. We all see things differently. More of that later.

So now you have had an illustration of Show and Tell, and, my word, we'll be doing much more on it as the book progresses.

Let me just tell you that the essentials of the structural form were present in both our TELL and SHOW excerpts: characters, main (Martin) and secondary (Henry), plot or story line (Martin's journey to save his friends), theme or the deeper problem, (home life leading to selfishness and low self-esteem) motivation (or what the character wants), tension (problems/solutions/holding back) and exposition (or the colouring in of the storyline). The unique voice – a unified interpretation in this instance.

Why were they present? They have to be to produce fiction that does not confuse. In the excerpts it was only the method of exposition that was different.

We'll come to it, don't worry, because as we work through *The Writer's Springboard* we're going to unpick the threads of the tapestry of fiction, explore them, and then see how they're woven back together.

We'll do this through explanation, application and writing exercises. Very soon you'll understand how to create scenes that live and breathe, and resolve issues that make your fiction thought provoking.

Though I strongly suspect you were already saying as we looked at SHOW, oh yes, I can see the sense in that.

I must emphasis that this handbook contains my thoughts on the creative writing process, and other tutors will have their own ideas. There are many wonderful books and workshops on writing; use them, and take a bit from everyone. The most important thing is to enjoy the craft.

Take it at your own pace, and don't expect too much all at once. Give yourselves time to think and imagine, dawdle, and enjoy.

Chapter 1. What *is* fiction? An introduction to the components. Advice on stirring the creative imagination. A deeper exploration of SHOW.

OK, we've got our foot in the door, so let's open it a little further and ask ourselves what fiction is. Before we do, here's a word of advice - just read *The Writer's Springboard* don't try to learn it as you go through. I hope there's enough repetition within the book to reinforce your understanding. You should take the time to do the exercises.

What is fiction? Literature that's invented? Yes, I think that'll do, but there's more. Fiction should make sense of events. It should have a resonance for the reader. It should explore some universal human experience or problem. It should entertain and transport. It should do so using the writer's unique and original voice.

Let's look at this again. When have you read a headline and pondered – who, why, how, when, where, whatever possessed them? If a particular headline interests us we'll read on, seeking to make sense of the event, the characters involved, the 'journey' leading to the headline climax.

We ask ourselves: Why was the main character motivated to respond in this way? What had gone on in her/his life to create this response? Not just the immediate trigger, but what was the deeper cause, the problem or experience that we can all 'universally' understand. In other words what is the theme running beneath it all? What is their past, their back-story that makes sense of their present day actions?

On and on we go, exploring it in our imagination, asking questions; why, when, where, how, what, who?

As we do this, we are creating scenes in our mind. We are seeing the characters, faintly at first, but they become clearer the more we ponder, just as the children and I did with Martin.

As we mull over these headlines or news reports, what we're seeking to do is create:

A)   Characters. Living breathing characters with whom we can identify. Martin was the main character, Henry was second in importance – a secondary character. Mr Evans was there, but in a minor way.

B)   Plot. A story line that has a beginning, middle and an end. Martin's story line was to begin a journey to the school camp, and then to go on and try to save his friends, which he eventually does, and in so doing, saves his emotional self.

C)   Theme. The deeper universal human problem. Martin's was one of low self-esteem which manifested through selfishness. His low self-esteem was caused by his brother's bullying.

D)   Motivation. The 'want' behind the characters' actions. Martin wanted to get away from his problems by going to the school camp. Motivation manifested in smaller ways too. He wanted to stand at the window to get cool. Henry wanted him to sit down. The clash of wants caused tension.

E)   Tension. The problems and conflicts along the way. Think of all the problems that created tension in Martin's story. Not just the big scenes, like the crash, the struggle to save his friends and come to terms with his emotional problem, but the line by line tension of 'holding back' on the action, the clash of wants, the clash with his own kinder instincts, brought about by his lack of self-esteem.

F)   Exposition. The personalisation of the situation by creating scenes which involve fleshed out characters, the setting, whilst still progressing the story line.

These components are the essentials of fiction writing, and are common to all Western literature. These components are the bedrock, the template of all our fiction if we are to achieve clarity and accessibility.

But, if we all use this same structural form how do we make our work sound different, unique, and appealing? Take a moment to consider your favourite authors.

I love Laurie Lee, Nikki Gemmell, Alan Paton, H.G. Wells, H.E.Bates, Ian Rankin, Reginald Hill, Bernard Cornwell, Anne Tyler, Mike Gayle, Mary Wesley, Pete McCarthy, Fanny Flagg, Barry Unsworth, Katie Fforde,

Isabel Losada, Elizabeth Buchan, Alexander McCall Smith, M.C. Beaton, David Mitchell, David Evans, James Lee Burke and the black women writers, the New World writers, on and on the list goes. But why do I like them? It's the way in which he or she perceives a situation, drawing on unique originality to create something 'different' within the common structure. In other words, in order to be fulfilled as writers, and to stand out, we need to access our creative imagination, and unearth our unique voice, honing our powers of empathy, therefore enabling us to get into the skins of our characters, and create living breathing exposition.

So there's a final and crucial essential.

G) Unique Voice

How do we find this voice? We use a series of rather enjoyable exercises that are designed to stimulate imagination and encourage empathy. I would like you to work on some of these from today and throughout this handbook as they will help on your writing journey.
The following ideas form the basis of *Writing Awake the Dreamweaver* but if you haven't read it, don't worry, the following advice will provide a foundation for *The Writer's Springboard*

To begin with, give yourselves the gift of time, which is perhaps the last thing we ever allow ourselves. But it's essential.

Each day:

1. Write for 20 minutes - the Daily Pages.

The Daily Pages are free writing, or in other words, stream of consciousness writing, and have been around for some time. They are not unique to me by any means. Stream of consciousness is just as it sounds - you let whatever is in your mind pour out onto the paper - without heed to punctuation or spelling. The Daily Pages stir your unconscious. They reinforce the habit of writing, and help remove inhibitions and self-consciousness. They lead to self-awareness and self-esteem.

I wake in the morning and pick up a pen or pencil and write for 20 minutes. I usually manage two pages, but it can be more, or less. Incidentally, you might decide it's better to write the Daily Pages later in the day. That's fine. Make up your own mind but that moment between sleep and wakefulness is extraordinarily fruitful. It's a time before inhibitions and the day's armour are fully in place.

If you find it difficult to get going, try listening to what is going on around you. Maybe there's a clock ticking. So say so. What else has ticked in your life? Maybe it's Uncle Henry's jaw? Not ticked, but clicked. Let your mind trawl. Roam amongst the memories held in your unconscious.

Or write about the pen in your hand. How does it feel? Let these small things lead you on to other observations, memories, feelings.

Feel free to write about whatever comes into your head. You might rage about a row you had the night before, or enjoy again a moment of triumph, or a dream, or an overheard conversation. Whatever comes into your head, let it stream out on the page. Let yourself feel the emotions in their raw state.

You might ask yourself questions, and not know the answers. That's OK. Say so. The day might come when you have the answer. You might show a nasty side of yourself. So what? We've all got one, but have been trained to hide it, in order to fit into society. Quite right too, we can't have everyone going around letting it all hang out. But not all your characters will be good and even the praiseworthy ones will be flawed in some way and have less than acceptable emotions. We're after a sense of reality, remember. So, get in touch with every facet of yourself. Your words will be quite safe.

Why? When you have completed the pages you will **destroy** them. *'Yer what?'*

You heard, **destroy** them. And this step is my own invention. In the Daily Pages you will only reveal the deep truths about yourself and your experiences if you are safe in the knowledge that no-one else can ever read them. If you don't destroy these pages, you will unconsciously censor yourself. I don't want you to feel inhibited in anyway. I want you to peel back the layers of conditioning and reclaim your unique voice and your creative force, for it is this that will make your structured writing vibrant and alive. I want you to remember experiences and feelings in order to encourage your ability to empathise; to put yourself in the bodies of your characters; the good, the bad and the ugly. Trust me, we'll all have been these at one time or another. No-one is perfect. I want you to be able to transcend the boundaries of your existing empathy because you will find yourself writing outside your own experiences a great deal of the time. You will have to imagine/empathise with emotions and reactions.

Nikki Gemmell, the 'anonymous' author of The Bride Stripped Bare said anonymity made her reckless. I want you to be just that, reckless, abandoned in your remembrance.

2. 20 minutes thinking time.

Later in the day, I would like you to put aside 20 minutes to concentrate on an action you are carrying out.

To kick off, I would like you to write your name with the hand you don't normally use. Note the action, and how it feels; the arrangement of your body, of your arm, your fingers on the pencil. Such detail, such conscious action, will force you to slow down, and make you 'stay in the moment', the facility needed for creating scenes. It will help you to note conscious actions when you are carrying out other daily tasks in those 20 minutes. Note also any emotions or memories the action triggers.

Then when you've done that, and thought about it, change to your normal writing hand and write about your name. What is it? Why did your parents choose it – was it for family reasons, did it cause trouble? Who actually chose it? When did they choose it? How did they choose it? Where was this? These are the questions writers must get used to asking themselves as they struggle to work out characters, the complexity of relationship interactions, plot, motivation, tension etc. just as the children and I did when exploring Martin's précis.

Now you've tried asking yourself these questions, and been introduced to the idea of examining an action, and staying in the moment whilst doing so, let's look at a few other ideas.

Try examining the task of ironing. How do you hold the iron? How do you iron? Notice the weight of the iron, the muscles being used. Let your mind stray, let it daydream which is so often the moment when inspiration pounces. You might think of the first time you saw your mother ironing - the smell of the clothes. Yes, that's right, use your senses. Then ask the questions. When was wash-day as a child, as an adult? Why was one day set aside, if it was? How was the wash done? What clothes, what washing machine? Where was it done? Try interweaving these memories, and perhaps thoughts of the future, into the detail of your ironing action, just as we did in the SHOW excerpt with Martin.

You can then think of noting how your action and stance changes with your mood. How differently do you iron if you are angry, sad, joyous and so on? If angry, is your grip tighter, your shirt ironing heedless? Do you **want** to iron badly, or to put it another way, are you **motivated** to iron badly? Keep examining how, on different days, your actions reflect your inner mood. It is through using action and consequently body language that you can bring to life some emotion in a scene without having to 'tell' or explain it, but SHOW it. You see, body language is as valuable as verbal language.

I want you to get used to asking questions of yourself and the world. I want you to get into the habit of asking who, what, why, how, when, where? I want you to see, hear, taste, smell, touch and remember and observe. It's along this road that empathy lies, and without it, your work will not live. Empathy will make your readers say, *'Yes, right. That's how it is.'* And for a moment they won't be so alone, they will have entered a world created by your unique voice and perception.

3. 30 minutes writing time on a given subject.

In ***Writing Awake the Dreamweaver*** I suggested a series of writing exercises that were designed to stimulate the imagination, encourage empathy, let you see scenes, and use the common structure.

I suggested that an exercise should be chosen in the morning, and thought about during the day in order to give the mind a chance to do some work behind the scenes. You'll find that our mind ticks away throughout the day, and when the moment comes to write, the creative imagination will produce something exciting. Remember what I said about symbolism just happening. Well, this is the same system.

Here are some exercises you might like to try. Write up each one.

1. Let's go back to childhood, and the games you played. Maybe you were racing across an imaginary plain with your mates, just riding along, when something happened to bring about a change. Perhaps a rustler fired on you

all. You had to make a decision whether to pursue, perhaps to rescue someone they'd taken, or not. Perhaps there was some discussion between you and the others in the gang, those of you who weren't 'on the other side'. Off you'd go, in pursuit of a goal, one of you leading your gang forward, overcoming difficulties until the situation was resolved in some way. Or maybe it was a different game. You were serving tea to imaginary guests. I bet your could almost taste that tea, and the sandwiches, and see the people you were entertaining. You were **there.** Be there again, as that small person.

2. Let's look at another scenario and take it a step further, asking ourselves who, why, what, where, when, how questions. Perhaps you were playing shops and had to buy something. Why did you ask for something? Why that particular one? Go on, push your imagination. Is it for you as a forbidden treat? If so, why is it forbidden, and why are you rebelling against the ruling? How do you ask for it, if it's a forbidden treat? Won't the shopkeeper know? How do you pretend it's OK? What would the shopkeeper say? And so on, and so on. Or is it later in life? It's up to you.

3. Or are you buying a gift for someone else? Why? Do they need cheering up? Why? Who are they? What is the gift? When is this? Where is this?

4. Here's another. Still in your childhood, write about a contemporary you disliked. Ask yourself why. Ask how your dislike manifested. Where did you play? Put yourself back there. Did you sit on the pavement, all of the gang? We did. It drove our mothers mad. Do you regret your behaviour towards your contemporary? Study the ins and outs of the situation. Let your mind roam. It might come up with forgotten feelings and memories. Be honest. Try to forget that we were told as children not to be unpleasant, or criticise, or notice imperfections, or make comment. As writers we need to remove these constraints. Otherwise, how are we to get inside our characters, those who are bad as well as good, and portray them as believable people?

5. When were you lost as a child? If you were never lost, try to imagine that you were. Be the height of a small child again, seeing legs, and shop counters, but no mum, or dad. How does it feel? Go on, actually get down at that height. Try to recapture the details, the body language. How did you behave when you were anxious and frightened? What were you doing when it happened? Did you bite your nails? Who helped you? When was this? Why were you there? Why did you get lost? What distracted you?

Remember that it's the details that can help whoosh your writing straight into a reader's heart and memory and aid identification.

6. Try this one. Did you ever go to the cinema and have to sit on prickly seats? Did you complain? How? Did you whisper and grumble? What did you actually say and to whom? What was the reply? Did someone in the seat behind tell you to *'Shut up.'* How did that make you feel?

Go on thinking of things to ask yourself, using the questions all writers ask themselves. When? Why? Where? Who? How? What? Remember how it worked well in the SHOW scene with Martin.

7. Here are a few others to work with. When were you thwarted? When did you thwart someone? Remember the feelings inherent in both. Did you feel resentment when being thwarted? Or anger? Did you feel guilt when thwarting, or was it satisfaction? Be honest. Be back in yourself, and if you can't remember the details, imagine how you would have felt.

8. Try this. When have you been offered an opportunity and turned it down? What moment or point of change either offered, or forced upon you, have you turned away from, one that would take you out of your normal world, your comfort zone, onto a different path, a different journey? After the initial hesitation/refusal, did you accept? Why do you think you accepted? What did you want to change – deep down, or what difference did the forced change make to your life? Presumably there were good and bad moments, and a general development in you as a person.

Are you getting the idea? Think up other writing exercises to stir memories of your past, awaken your senses, your imagination, your **Dreamweaver.** None of these exercises are a waste of time or effort. An ancient Chinese poet felt that re-creating something in words is like being alive twice.

In case we get too obsessed with studying our own navels, take time also to observe the ballets going on around you. Observe the relationships you see at the next café table, the body language, the chatting, or lack of. Observe those you pass in the streets, or sit near on buses or trains. Get used to being aware of what is going on around you, see the sub-text of people's conversations and body language. By this I mean that if there is a couple at the next table and she is chatting and he is clearly not listening, try and see how you **know** he's not listening. If you overhear a conversation, try and work out what is behind, or the sub-text of, the actual language, if things seem a bit tense.

We're now going to embark on a larger project, but using the same tools - why, how, what etc. using imagination, but hopefully incorporating memory as well. This exercise might take you some while, even a few days. Read through the task, and then **think**. There's no hurry. Writers must learn to think and live with a scenario to make it work well. When you're ready, get writing.

9. I want you to imagine yourself on a shingle beach. It can be winter or summer, balmy weather or stormy. You are the creator – decide for yourself. I want you to BE there, and to stay in the moment.

So take one step. Feel your foot in its shoe, and **sink** into the shingle. Does your heel sink first? Go on, get up and take a pace, and imagine that you are placing a foot into those small stones. How do you *actually* do it? Then take another step.

Remember what we said about tension. Each step on shingle is a struggle. The shingle seems to slip away from you, you are struggling to go forward and feel all the time that you are slipping back. Maybe you should slip, before correcting yourself. There you go, a bit of tension already, a problem which is overcome. BE there, doing it. Stay in the moment. What does this first, then second step feel like?

Now think again. Imagine you are barefoot this time. You will feel the stones digging and rolling beneath your feet. Does that remind you of a childhood time? Does it symbolise something that's going on in your life, something that is hurting you, slipping away from you? Just hint at it as you take the first, then second step. Don't say everything. Hold back as we did with Martin.

Go back to shoes. A stone could slip in. How do you remove it? Do you stand on one foot and wobble about, wishing you had someone to support you? Where is that someone? Does it make you cross that he or she isn't here?

Now revert to your preference, shoes or barefoot for the rest of the exercise.

What is going on around you? Can you feel the wind, the sun? Is the breeze tugging at your clothes? What clothes? Don't just list them, but SHOW us as the weather messes about with them. Is the wind tugging at your hair? Does it go across your eyes, block your vision momentarily. And so on. Go on, just be there, in this moment, in this scene, as we were with Martin at the window. He felt the dust, but he compared the wide open spaces to his tenement home environment. Use one thing to do two things. Layer it, show us your voice. It will be different to everyone else who is doing this exercise, because you are accessing the real you. Take as long as you like taking these two steps.

When you are ready, continue with the next stage.

10.   You have taken a few more steps, and have reached a breakwater or groyne. It is a man-made fence-like structure that goes down into the sea, and usually occurs at regular intervals to break up the wave force, and stop beach erosion. If you want to picture it properly go to the library, or find one on the internet, or better still, take a day out and go to a beach. Try climbing over one, noticing all the details of the groyne and the setting, your actions, feelings, and thoughts. Then reward yourself with an ice cream.

The one in the exercise is pretty old and broken down, and what's more, it's blocking your way, causing a problem that needs to be overcome. Remember Martin's story, and how we held back with the crash.

I want you to climb over this structure. I want you to take your time. It should have some difficulties. Don't explain, but SHOW us what you're doing. You might slip, or struggle to find a toehold, a handhold, or both. Perhaps there are barnacles that graze, or seaweed that is slippery. I want you to get over and feel a sense of achievement. You wanted help, but managed without it. Write this up.

Onto the next stage.

11.   This time, I want you to backtrack. Let's add another layer to the scene. Read through the task, and then give yourself time to think, and your creative imagination will come up with helpful moments for your scene.

Go back to where you are approaching the breakwater. I want you to hear someone calling you. Just stay in the moment, be there. You turn. It is just the person you didn't want, or perhaps hoped to see. You have a choice. You watch as they hurry across the shingle from the car park just at the edge of the beach. You take the first step to climbing over the breakwater while they're heading towards you. Remember your senses. You will be able to tell if they start to run. How? 'ear 'ear. Yes, you'll hear them.

The other person arrives, I want you to SHOW the relationship between the two of you, by the way in which the other person does, or doesn't help you to climb the breakwater and your reaction to them. How do they help you? Do they just do it? Whether you want them to or not? If they insist when you say you don't want their help, what does that say about the relationship between you? If you are pleased to see them, what has gone on for you to be on the beach alone? If you are not pleased, why? How are you going to hint at this? If they don't help but you want them too, how is this made clear? Do you use interior monologue, or in other words thought, or dialogue, or/and body language? Whatever the atmosphere, what is the reason for the problem? Just be there. Think it through.

That's the end of that part of the exercise. Onto the next stage.

12. As you climb the breakwater you see, or perhaps hear to begin with, a young woman running out from the dunes in the near distance down onto the beach. She is being chased by a man. She shouts at you. 'Don't let him get me.' Meanwhile the man is shouting, 'Stop her.' What do you want to do?

I want the person who joined you at the breakwater to be trying to stop you getting involved. I want you to listen to them, hesitate and then make your decision to get involved, either by helping the chaser or the chased.

This final stage will probably take quite a long time to sort out. Remember to stay in the moment, to BE there, in your body. How do you stop the girl, or do you let her go? How do you overcome the interference from your friend/husband/lover? Why do you go against him or her? What's the background to this? Why do you take a decision to change things in this way? Because change things you most certainly will, if you defy this person who is already in your life. Where will you try and stop the girl, or not stop her? We know when, because we're already with you.

There will be a lot of conflict in this final part of the scene - conflict between you and the person who is second in importance in the scene (your friend, lover, mother, father, husband, child), and conflict when you do get involved. Do you stop the girl, or the man? How do you make your choice?

It's interesting because we are inclined to believe that a young girl being chased by a man is the victim but is she really? Stay in the moment and create this scene.

Whatever your decision, there will be consequences. If you stop the wrong person, there are consequences. If you stop the right person, there are consequences. Not just the consequences of your actions on the level concerning the girl or man, but deeper consequences because you have just defied an important person in your life. This would indicate that there was something wrong in the first place for this person to try and influence you, and for you to respect them so little that you defy them. In other words, there is an emotional human problem or theme.

In this scenario there is the potential for a story. The consequences of your decision can lead to a plot concerning the girl or the chaser, in which your personal relationship problems can develop and resolve alongside.

So, here you are, creating scenes, staying in the moment, and before you know where you are, you've reached a point where you could turn this into a story or a novel

We will be doing much more on SHOW, and on methods of digging back into the characters' world to make the scenes work and progress the plot, as the handbook continues. But what a lot you've achieved already, even though the door has only opened a few more inches.

In Chapter 2 we'll be looking at the essential structural form to which you need to adhere, if you are to achieve an accessible vehicle to carry your living breathing characters and scenes.

I'm a great believer in celebrating achievement. So why not take this as a natural break and go out and have a treat. Do something you want to do, so you come back to the next chapter refreshed.

Chapter 2. The Structural Components in their entirety. Plot, characters, motivation, theme, tension, exposition, original voice. An exploration of each component. Their usage within Cinderella.

There is only one common structural form in use in the Western writing world. It was contained in the first fairy story to which we listened, in all the books and short stories we've read, the films and stage plays we've seen, the radio plays we've heard. We know it, but need to be reminded of it.

For our fiction to be instantly accessible to our readers, we need to use this common structural form. We need then to make it our own, by creating scenes in our own voice. This is something you have already done in Chapter 1, and will do again. A word of warning - some of you might consider that you are experimentalist writers, ones that need to break rules. In order to break rules, you must know them.

We are going to look at the common structural form in stages.

1.   The components of the common structural form.
2.   An exploration of each component.
3.   Their usage within a piece of fiction.

1   THE COMPONENTS OF THE COMMON STRUCTURAL FORM

Plot (+ sub-plot)

Characters

Motivation

Theme

Tension/conflict

Exposition

Unique Voice

2. An exploration of each component. I say again, that I think it's best to just read through. At the end of the chapter, we'll be seeing the components at work in Cinderella. Don't try and understand it all at once.

THE COMPONENTS OF THE COMMON STRUCTURAL FORM

PLOT

Plot is the storyline or vehicle that carries all the other components: Characters, motivation, theme, tension/conflict, exposition, and our unique voice.

The plot has one common shape.

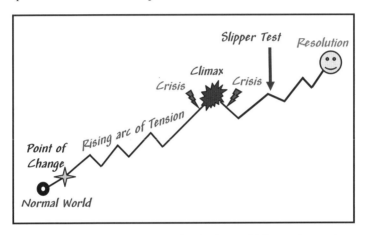

We can break it down initially into a beginning, middle, and an end.

Let's look at Martin's story.
1. Boy wants to go to summer camp and escape his life
2. Boy is thwarted by events from achieving his aim.
3. Boy arrives at summer camp and on the journey, comes to terms with his life.

The **beginning** of a story line is set in the main character's normal world, but at a point of change. Once the main character has accepted the challenge or opportunity presented at this point of change he or she embarks on a journey to achieve their aim. This journey involves a rising arc of tension.

Think of you/your character at the breakwater, making a decision to defy the wishes of their friend, lover or whatever. We started in the character's normal world as things stand at the moment, and almost immediately we were at a point of change – the decision that would change the main character's journey through life. So, for the purpose of fiction and tension, do you defy your friend immediately? No, but after a bit of shilly shallying you make up your mind to defy and to help someone else. That point of change has consequences that take you on an arc of tension towards the resolution.

But what happens on that arc of tension?

Let's consider Martin in the desert. We are shown his normal world which is that of a rebellious outsider, someone who barely cares about anyone or anything and whose home life is less than perfect. Then the bus bursts a tyre. Martin is thrown out. We're at the point of change. Once the bus is in the ravine, Martin is the only one who can go for help. Mr Evans yells up that the quickest way is over the escarpment, it is too far by road. Martin will hesitate – still in the point of change. Who wouldn't? It's a plausible reaction. Remember how you/your character had to pluck up courage to defy your friend/foe at the breakwater. Remember the task I set in Chapter 1, asking you to recapture a moment when you were offered an opportunity and hesitated to leave your comfort zone. Why? Fear probably.

Martin is frightened. He doesn't think he can make it, and why should he endanger himself, for them? It is only when he hears that Henry is hurt that we, the reader, know he might accept the challenge. Be aware that we've already seen the hint of a glimmer of 'good' in Martin on the bus when he clearly felt something approaching friendship for the other outsider, Henry with the gammy leg.

On top of Martin's hesitation at the point of change, is the urgency of the situation. Not only are the others trapped in rising heat, but Henry needs help. It is to be a race against time to get medical help. As with all good fiction, there's the potential for several strands of tension.

Off Martin goes on the **Rising Arc of Tension.** Take a look at the graph again. See that it takes up approximately two thirds of the story line and involves overcoming challenges and obstacles as the main character proceeds on his/her journey.

Martin's journey is comprised of many difficulties. These are a) environment – the escarpment. b) another person maybe, (it would help with scene building to introduce another character for interaction between the two. Maybe another kid manages to scramble out of the ravine, someone Martin dislikes, a bully who wants all the glory but is found wanting – he could symbolise Martin's struggle against his brother. This is the wonderful thing about fiction – you can go back and add to the original idea to improve it). c) Most importantly, Martin must overcome the weaknesses and problems within himself as well as those thrown up by the environment and his opponent, or antagonist, just as we do in real life. And this is why your readers will stay with you.

Let's look at the potential for creating scenes along this journey. At the start, it would be appropriate for the other boy to bully his way into leadership as they trudge towards the foot of the escarpment. Let's try to outline a scene which can show the beginning of the **turning** of the tables.

They reach the bottom of the escarpment and start up and Martin's confidence grows because he is the more able - to his own surprise. You would need to show this. Perhaps the opponent barges up the wrong slope, calling Martin to follow. Martin has seen a better way and takes it, defying his 'leader'. The leader has to come back when his route reaches a dead end, and follow Martin. How symbolic is that? Are you getting the idea? But this is only the beginning of the change. The leader would take control again and it is only as they overcome more obstacles that Martin's confidence increases as the bully's decreases until Martin is now the leader. Martin is in control because he is the better and more capable person. The reader sees this development and empathises. Martin is developing for our sakes, as well as his own. We are identifying with him.

Finally they reach almost to the top of the escarpment. Mindful of the need for tension, and our graph, let's make ourselves two thirds of the way through the story line. We're at the 3 x Cs. Crisis-Climax-Crisis.

We need a big crisis as they almost reach the top of the escarpment and what seems to be the end of their problems.

Let's have the bully slipping down to almost halfway again, hurting his leg in the process. So near and yet so far. Yes, that's a big enough A **crisis**, just as they're on the point of success. You can see how fiction demands that you 'hold back' all the time.

To symbolise the absolute change in power you could have Martin facing another decision. Having started character development on the climb up (with Martin focussed on saving those in the bus), he now has to make a decision – to go on alone and save them, or go back and save the bully as well. Of course, he climbs back down to him, and then has to half carry him up the escarpment, and make it to the top. At this point they have reached the **Climax**. Martin's story line problem seems solved and perhaps his emotional inner problem too, because there's the airfield where he can get help. Martin's self-esteem is improved; he has become the leader because he deserves it, he has coped. He has no need to be bullied anymore. Furthermore, we could make the bully grateful. At last they are friends and in this together.

But, with an eye to the graph, we need another Crisis. So let's see what we can produce.

Let's have them seeing the airfield. Oh no, there is a river in between, and we, the authors, invent a situation - Martin can't swim. The bully is injured. Is all lost?

For a moment all is at its worst. This is the darkest moment. Truly the achievement of Martin's aim is so near and yet so far.

Let's take a quick look at Cinderella for a moment just to see the 3Cs in action. The simplified plot of Cinderella: (It's always a good idea to simplify your plot. It helps the thinking process)

1. Girl wants to go to the ball 2. Girl struggles to achieve her aim of going to the ball with her family to show that she is loved and has resumed her rightful place. 3. Girl achieves her aim of going to the ball which leads to her finding love, and status.

Now for a more careful look at the shape of the plot.

There's Cinderella at the start of her story, in her normal world in the kitchen in rags. Then along comes a point of change – the invitation. Will she or won't she try and go to the ball as is her right? Finally she does decide to bargain with the step-mother and sisters. She is told that if she does all the chores she can join the family party. Off we go on a rising arc of tension as we follow Cinderella in her attempts to fulfil the tasks set by the Steps, tasks made more difficult by the obstacles they deliberately put in her way.

On the night of the ball, with all the chores accomplished, they renege. Cinderella cannot go to the ball after all. A big **crisis**. Then in comes the Fairy Godmother and all is well. Off Cinderella goes and is the belle of the ball. The **climax**. Then the clock strikes 12. Oh no. The third C. Another **crisis**. At the height of success, all seems lost as Cinderella flees in rags from her Prince, and the world that is rightfully hers. It is her darkest moment.

So it is with Martin too. We're at the third C stage, the **crisis.**

Let's recap. He's reached the top and sees the airfield, it doesn't look far but oh no, there's a river between him and it, and he can't swim, and he's got the injured friend. Will Martin despair, give up. Has he really developed as a person as the plot would suggest? Let's outline a scene. He's hot and tired and worn out, and very thirsty. What little water he has he's just given to his companion. For a moment he gives into despair, but his companion's need, and the needs of those in the bus stir him, and one other thing enters the scene; his brother's words in interior monologue. Don't be a wimp. But it's not disparaging in his head this time, it's helpful. It spurs him on. So here we incorporate various levels - his past, his present, and the future, **and** the physical and emotional levels. He's re-interpreting his life from this new position of balance. He accepts the challenge and heads with his companion for the river. The 3rd C has been overcome.

Don't try and remember all this, just read through. We'll be doing this again later.

We're into the last third of the story now. Can Martin show that he's developed sufficiently to deserve our involvement? Let's move on now to the river, to the 'Slipper, or Confirmatory Test'.

Why Slipper Test?

During Cinderella's darkest moment, she drops her glass slipper. After some nail biting sessions in the home of Cinderella, during which we feel the Prince will never find Cinderella, he reaches her house. Of course the Steps try and ram their little tootsies into the slipper, to no avail. And here we come to the Slipper or confirmatory test. Will Cinders make sure she tries on that slipper, in order to achieve her aim of being loved?

Will Martin find a way to get over the river, once he reaches it? Of course he will, and in so doing, save the others and achieve his aim of staying at school camp. A resolution at last. But more than merely arriving as school camp, Martin has definitely found self-esteem and the esteem of others. We know he won't go back to anger and resentment, we know he'll be able to overcome his brother's bullying as he overcame his travelling companion's.

The resolution need not tidy things up completely, but there should be a way forward for the main character.

The shape we have just been exploring is the basic shape of our fiction. It is the shape your shingle beach scene has begun to take. Let's recap. On the beach you have reached the point of change, and your involvement in the girl, or pursuing man's life, will take you onto the rising arc of tension. Just to reinforce the shape, think of a stage play. Where does the interval come? Usually two thirds of the way through.

A point to bear in mind, and one we will look at more closely, is that a short story will usually stop at the crisis, climax. It has 2Cs, not three, and moves onto the resolution immediately afterwards. We will also discuss the sub-plot later. Let's not overload the brainbox quite yet.

Let's look at the diagram again. You will see that the line is jagged. This is to indicate numerous obstacles. But you already know that.

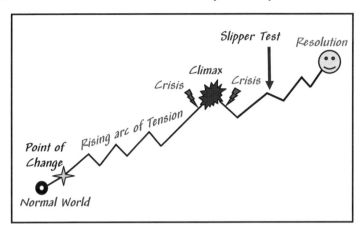

This is because the journey of your main character is always full of tension, created by obstacles. Let's take another look at Martin in the SHOW scene. Right at the start, even in small ways, we had tension. Not only were there big problems like the tyre bursting, the bus spinning and Martin falling out, but we had Henry drawing attention to the fact that Mr Evans might see him and Martin would get everyone into trouble. Will he, won't he see him or not? It's a form of tension. Evans doesn't. The problem is over. Then Henry attempts to clutch Martin's leg in order to help him. Will he, won't he succeed? His hand slips slowly. Not too quickly, let's hold back and keep the tension up. You will remember that we don't have Martin flying out straight away. The bus spins but the tension build up takes its time. It keeps us reading. Do note, however, that it wasn't all tension and bad temper. There was that moment of light when Martin thought kindly of Henry, and his pleasure at the scenery. Ups and downs, remember.

We'll look at tension more closely on and off throughout the book. Just take a moment to think of the childhood game of riding across the desert after rustlers. There was a beginning, middle and an end. In other words, there was a general build towards a resolution, during which lots of obstacles were overcome. It's the vehicle or plot, or story, which has a common shape, one that carries the common structural components. Another way of thinking about the plot, is to compare it to a cake tin, in which all the components are stirred together to create a wonderful mix.

Let's keep the cake tin analogy in mind and consider the characters as the flour. Let me just say that you know all this, because you've lived in a world where you have been aware of fiction in its myriad forms. I'm just bringing this knowledge to the forefront of your minds.

MOTIVATION – THE SUGAR

Motivation, or want or aim, is the driving force that carries the character through to the end. It is the desire to achieve their goal. Cinderella's motivation is to want to go to the ball to prove that she's loved and restored to her rightful position. Her step-family's want or motivation is to keep her away from the ball in case she achieves her rightful place. Let's take the film Erin Brokovitch. Do watch it. Erin's motivation is to find a job that will support her kids. As the film progresses, her motivation grows to 'want' to succeed against a powerful corporation for the sake of the people it is destroying. The corporation's motivation is to prevent her succeeding. Be aware that motivation can grow and develop.

Martin's motivation is to go to summer camp, at first. This motivation changes to wanting to save Henry, and the others, and for them all to be at summer camp.

However, motivation/want is rather empty as it stands. I remember when growing up that it was considered selfish to 'want'. It was what you 'needed' that mattered. In the same way, within fiction the 'want' needs something deeper to underpin it, some psychological truth, some universal human emotional problem or experience to validate the 'want'. In other words, it needs a theme.

Exercises

When were you motivated to pursue a course of action recently? What did you want? A new kitchen? Reasonable behaviour from others? A new coat? Write about the measures you took or are taking to achieve your aim.

What was the reasoning behind this? Was it essentially practical, or could you as a writer think of something that could underpin this motivation in a protagonist?

THEME – THE MARGARINE

The theme is the idea, or universal human experience or problem the writer is exploring. It could be injustice (Cinderella) or lack of self-esteem (Martin) The theme can be revenge, redemption, jealousy, a need to come to terms with the past. It can be a need to redress the balance of power in relationships, or guilt. Whatever you want it to be.

We are alerted to the theme of **injustice** in Cinderella right from the start. There she is toiling away in her rags to general abuse and lack of gratitude when the invitation comes. It becomes clear that Cinderella is not any old maid, but the Count's real daughter. Immediately we are engaged. This is outrageous. After all, haven't we all at some time or other been the victim of injustice, big or small. This is the need underlying Cinderella's motivation. If she goes to the ball she'll be seen to have been restored to her rightful place. She'll be part of the family, and her family will love her at last, or at the very least she hopes that she'll find love at the ball. And injustice will have been addressed.

Similarly with Erin Brokovitch. The film opens as the main character, Erin Brokovitch struggles through a job interview, fails to land the position, drives away, goes through a **green** light and is hit side on by a car that shot the lights. In the subsequent court case she is defeated because she appears to be a tart, with a dubious home life, whilst the perpetrator is a respected doctor, who therefore couldn't be in the wrong. I beg your pardon? Her journey then becomes more interesting. Why? Her motivation is underpinned by the theme. Instead of just wanting to keep a job to financially underpin her life, she is motivated to address **injustice**, a theme born out of her own experiences, and what's more we can empathise, as most of us have been the victim of injustice at one time or another.

Can you see that the theme is all important? It is what gives the story its relevance to the readers' lives. It's what they identify with. Remember we'll use the Zigzag Path to help you find yours. Basically, the plot and the characters are the devices the writer uses to explore the theme. This underlines its importance. Without it, you have nothing.

Exercises.

Try to identify the theme in the fiction you are reading or watching this week.

Try to identify the theme underlying the fiction you have already written.

Is it there?

Is it the same in every piece? It often is – a writer writes out of his or her own experience or emotional past.

Look at pictures in magazines, those that appear in Sunday supplements. Imagine the theme underlying the composition of the characters. What is it really about?

CHARACTERS – THE FLOUR

Protagonists, Secondary Characters, Minor Characters.

There is usually only one main character. It is his or her journey. The main character is called the protagonist from the Greek for 1st combatant. There are usually one or more secondary characters. These are second in importance to the main character, or protagonist, and sometimes carry a sub-plot (in a novel). Martin was the main character in our desert story. You were the main character in your shingle beach scenario.

The role of a secondary character is to facilitate or hinder the protagonist's journey. They can be mentors or antagonists. These roles can change within a character. Characters can begin as antagonists, (those who oppose) and become mentors, (supporters) or the other way round. Think of Martin. His as yet nameless 'rescue' companion is a secondary character, and starts as antagonist and could easily end up becoming a mentor, especially if their relationship develops to the extent where they help one another across the river.

32

There are minor characters – the spear carriers. They can also be mentors or antagonists, but are usually a device to move the plot forward, or reveal some piece of information. For instance, they can bring a message into the boardroom, and the reaction of the Chairman can reveal something about the plot. Mr Evans was a minor character in Martin's story. He was there on the bus, but not second in importance. Henry and the nameless companion are secondary characters.

Characters are devices to explore your theme and story, but devices with whom the reader has to identify. Characters personalise the skeleton of the story line.

In particular, the readers have, at least, to understand and grow to like, admire, or sympathise with the hero or heroine. The main character/protagonist needs to be fighting for something with which the reader can identify.

It is not enough for the reader to be involved only with the protagonist. They must also understand the secondary characters, even the baddies. You must avoid stereotyping. Hardly anyone is born good or bad, there should be a reason for an antagonist's behaviour; one that is plausible and which becomes clear as the story progresses. Remember that word – plausible.

This is why it is important that you work on your own experiences in order to empathise with the characters you create. You must remember times when you were less than pleasant, those times when you bullied, were unfair. But also when you were bullied, received injustice, or any other possible themes you might consider exploring.

If there were no specific characters to identify with, we would be left with something resembling a business report about a situation, and nothing with which to empathise. Think again of Cinderella's plot.

1. Girl wants to go to the ball
2. Girl struggles to achieve her aim of going to the ball with her family to show that she is loved and returned to her rightful place.
3. Girl achieves her aim of going to the ball which leads to her finding love, and status.

Without specific characters this scenario is a skeleton. One that is mildly interesting, but not involving because we're not identifying with the girl. We're not **personalising** the event.

Let me reiterate that the protagonist drives the event. As the author, you have to get inside that character, become them. The story has to revolve around the motivation and theme of the main character. Everything you devise must be relevant to that character. Even the secondary characters must be relevant to that character.

In order to create that character you can sit down and draw up a list of her/his looks, their past, present, their habits, relations, friends, interests and so on. I find it hard to do this in the cold light of day. I need to work together with theme, motivation, plot, and allow the character to grow in context. I use my Zigzag Path for this. We will arrive at that in due course, and I'm sure you'll find it takes a lot of the '*Oh blimey, how can I just conjure up a character?*' out of the situation. We'll use the why, what, who, when, where, how questions you have already used in Chapter 1.

You know you can do it, so just relax and trust yourself. We use stream of consciousness and you've already worked on this so you'll find it quite painless.

For now let's just look more carefully at the roles our main characters, secondary and minor fulfil to help consolidate your understanding.

Who and what is Cinderella, that beguiling mistreated young woman who is the victim of great injustice?

Cinderella is the protagonist. It is her journey. It is a journey to which everything else must be relevant. The writer must not be tempted to deviate from the protagonist's motivation and theme. They must get from the opening page to the resolution.

Let's go back to Martin's story for a moment. We knew his name, and Henry's, even that of Mr Evans. I deliberately gave his travelling companion no name. I wanted to prove to you how it would have brought him to life to have had one, even in the synopsis type situation in which we met him.

The breakwater scene. Wouldn't it have been better to name and personalise the protagonist's friend/foe, the one the protagonist ended up defying?

34

Think of Cinderella again. It's Cinderella with whom we identify. It's Cinderella who carries our hopes as well as her own as she struggles towards triumph.

Let's look at another example. What about the film Erin Brokovitch? Where would that story have been without the feisty Erin, with whom we identify as she struggles to overcome a multitude of problems? Without her it would have been a discussion of an issue or event - that of the betrayal of a firm towards its employees.

We might have tutted, but I suggest that we wouldn't have become totally involved. With Erin driving the story, however it became my fight too as she fought her private and professional battles and grew in the process. I was there, my sense of empowerment growing as hers grew. Her frustration at injustice, personal and professional, was mine as her motivation clashed with the motivation of others, building the tension almost unbearably. But, good grief, the girl did it. It made me feel I could do something similar as she powered forward, striving to bring justice to the employees, and to herself.

Let's break down the facets of tension that make the protagonist's journey more difficult.

These facets of tension are antagonists.

Antagonists can be

a) Other characters
b) Something within the protagonist
c) Environmental obstacles.
d) All three (and frequently are)

We've seen this at work in Martin's story. His **brother's words** stopped him from sitting down. Perhaps he perceives **Henry** as an antagonist who is trying to remove him from the cooling wind. He sees **Mr Evans** as one, for he is the human face of all the rules Martin is determined to break. Then there is the **travelling companion.** Then there is the **environment** - the escarpment, the river. Then his **inner conflict** - lack of self-esteem that makes him doubt himself and causes so much of his selfishness.

So there is Martin, with all three rumbling along on the journey.

Antagonistic Secondary Characters in fiction.

Characters that take the antagonist role are secondary characters. They are of lesser importance than the protagonist. The antagonist's role is to thwart the protagonist. Antagonists can become mentors. As I've already said, Martin's 'rescue' companion, and here I'm going to give him a name, Alec, could help, even as Martin tries to get him up the escarpment when he is injured, and more so when they cross the river.

I chose the name Alec because it sounds and looks different to Martin. Matthew would have been too close to Martin, and could cause confusion. If you developed Alec into a mentor, then you would need to devise an alternative antagonist. In their case, the river would be enough, I think. But you must bear the need for alternative antagonists in mind.

Mentor role of Secondary Characters in fiction.

We've just mentioned them, so let's look at what they are in more detail. Think again of Cinderella and Erin Brokovitch. They both have mentors. All protagonists have mentors, or in other words helpers, just as we do in real life. In Cinderella there is the Fairy Godmother, (and Buttons in the pantomime version). In Erin Brokovitch there is her boyfriend, who ceases to be a mentor for a while. There's her lawyer who begins as mentor, then is momentarily antagonist as she tries to get a job with him, then again becomes her mentor though at one point she feels he's betrayed her.

Return for a moment to Martin and Alec. The gradual change from antagonist to mentor must be plausible. Alec would take time to change and that would coincide with Martin's development. Alec would revert to his old self, just as Martin will be tempted to do throughout his journey. Think of real life; change doesn't happen overnight. It's often two steps forward, one back as the character gets to grips with his problems. Keep it believable.

Let's look at the film Erin Brokovitch again. Erin's boss and the other members of staff are hardly mentors to begin with, but as she develops and shows her worth, they change. Their places as antagonists are taken by others:

a) Those who are damaging the environment and people.

b) Later members drafted onto Erin's team.

c) Some of those that Erin's firm is trying to help are antagonistic.

d) Her boyfriend and also her son become momentary antagonists.

Watch the film and see if you can see the changeovers. All these obstacles, and the overcoming of them, help the writer to develop the emotional maturing of the protagonist and perhaps the secondary characters **and keep us watching**. In this way there is more satisfaction in the resolution. 'Boy, do they deserve it,' we say.

As I've just said, mentors or antagonists can be portrayed as 'memory'. The memory of someone who influences the protagonist. In Martin's journey, thoughts of his brother, who we met during his interior monologue, could steer him towards aggression in his dealings with Alec. Had his brother been a mentor, it would have steered him in a different way.

I would suggest that we all have our own 'memory' mentors and antagonists so if we remember their roles in our lives we can use that experience in our fiction to bring depth and plausibility.

Now I don't want any panic about all this. We will be coming to the Zigzag Path shortly, which will help produce the characters you need, and their histories. And just think how much you have remembered about the stories you have read, that you didn't realise you knew. That's the key, you see. This isn't rocket science. You already know these components, if you have read and watched and listened to stories and dramas. We're just taking the tapestry apart and exploring it in detail, ready to put it together in the Zigzag Path.

You can also see how close fiction is to real life. We all know antagonists and mentors. We've taken antagonistic and mentor roles, or had them thrust upon us. We've been on the receiving end. That's why we can relate to them in fiction as readers and writers. We're on familiar territory.

I've just said that fiction is close to real life. Let me take another run at that. Yes, but there is one fundamental difference. Fiction takes just one main problem at a time in a person's life (or at least in the early stages of writing). It is much as a detective would dearly like to take one case at a time and resolve it, concentrating exclusively on it until a resolution is reached. With real life it's one darned thing after another and often several at one time.

Let's go back to Henry for just a moment. Henry is a secondary character within that early scene, but once we leave the bus we need to keep him in Martin's mind and dialogue if he's to continue in that role. Wouldn't it be good also to keep him firmly in our minds, and to see what's happening in the bus?

Henry has the opportunity to be a truly important secondary character if we gave him a sub-plot, within the crashed bus, to give us this view. Henry would have to have his own motivation and theme which could be to prove that though injured on top of having a gammy leg, he is as much a 'man' as the others – and by so doing, proving it to himself. Also he would want to prove that Martin can be trusted.

This sub-plot will have one main aim - for Henry and the others to survive until Martin brings help. So you can see that it is still bound to the protagonist's main problem. We'll look at sub-plots later.

We'll move onto another look at minor characters.

Minor characters in fiction.

Minor characters fulfil minor roles. They are the spear carriers of fiction if you like. These would be the mice that became footmen in Cinderella and the guy in charge of the records in Erin Brokovitch, and the other unimportant personnel in Erin's firm, or the waitress in the diner. They speak, they facilitate the scene. For example: The waitress takes Erin's order – the children have something, but Erin has nothing. She hasn't enough money, though she doesn't say this. We are being SHOWN that Erin is a good mother, a caring parent. (The waitress incidentally is acted by the real Erin Brokovitch). So the waitress did not need to be developed, but she did have a purpose. One that was relevant to the protagonist.

Minor characters need not be drawn in anything like the same detail as your main character. Their function is to A) interact with the main and secondary characters or/and B) to help the writer provide the reader with necessary information and /or C) to move the story along.

They must always be integral to the plot. If you can do without them, then do so. Ask yourself that question. Do I need him/her? Yes, I know, yet another question. Think of a hot air balloon. (No, not me). It can't take off with excess weight, and neither can your story.

Another example in fiction could be a doorman opening a door to show the arrogance of the person entering. They are there but only to show something about someone or the setting. It could be a baddy who backs up a major antagonist. It was Mr Evans in the opening scene.

Don't fret at any of this. Remember that I said we'd be examining everything again, in greater detail. If you want to do a few exercises, take time now, or come back to them later.

Exercises

Watch Erin Brokovitch

Pick out the minor characters in your reading of the moment. Pick out the protagonist and secondary characters. Are they mentors or antagonists? See how they alter, or not.

TENSION – THE BAKING POWDER

You have seen already how important it is to build up tension. To hold back, make things that little bit more difficult, so that you get that jagged line throughout the diagram. There are big obstacles such as Martin's escarpment, and smaller ones throughout each 'stay in the moment' scene, such as Henry saying that Mr Evans will be furious, and so we wonder if Martin will be seen. There are your efforts to get over the breakwater. You don't go in one great leap, you stay in the moment and scratch yourself on barnacles, or slip, or whatever. Plus, when you get the next stage with your antagonist joining you, there is that complication too.

Exercise.

I want you to play the game of Consequences with yourself. This is the scenario. A girl is trying to hail a cab. She is in danger of being late for an interview. I want you to provide Problems and Solutions. Or do this with a writing friend or group, and pass it between you.

I will start you off.

Problem: Girl eventually flags down a taxi. She reaches for the door. The handle is stuck.
Solution:
Problem:
Solution:
Problem:
She reaches the building 2 minutes late. Has she blown it? Have her experiences made her more determined to gain admission? Has she developed some resolve?

EXPOSITION – THE EGGS

Exposition can also be called characterisation. This is the means by which the writer turns the plot, the characters, the motivation and theme and tension into a living breathing believable and affecting world, by creating scenes that **show.** Exposition is your unique voice **showing** your story, and involves setting, dialogue, interior monologue, simile, metaphor, symbolism, pace, rhythm, point of view.

I am not going to give you exercises for this yet, beyond asking you to explore how the authors you are reading put flesh on the bones of the plot, how characters in the films, TV and stage dramas SHOW their feelings, and receive the feelings of others. We will be working in much greater detail on the devices of exposition soon.

UNIQUE VOICE

The unique voice is the perception you have about the story you are writing, or the cake you are baking. Only you know which flavour you will decide upon, how large it will be, how firmly you will beat the mixture, and whether it will be iced or not. You will make that cake, write that story, from the depths of who you are.

I think you're beginning to realise that once you start unearthing the real you, you will create your own scenario to every plot. For instance, if I asked everyone reading this handbook to re-create Cinderella using the basic plot, you would all create something different. Keep on with the imagination exercises, the recapturing of memory, the 'staying in the moment' everyday tasks.

Remember, we'll be covering all the points of structure again in yet another form, and seeing how it is applied.

ZIGZAG PATH – THE WOODEN SPOON

I will now mention the equivalent of the wooden spoon - The Zigzag Path. In my writing life it's what makes everything buzz, bubble and rise. It's what makes life easier. It's what makes all the above points far more accessible.

The Zigzag Path gets me started once I have an idea. It locates the history of the protagonist and **why** they are as they are. It defines **what** they are, it brings up the **who, how, when, where** of the plot. If I let my stream of consciousness run free, as you are teaching yourselves in your exercises and daily pages, it enables me to flow backwards, **and** forwards. My imagination produces the threads I need, the scenes, the setting, snatches of dialogue. It's effortless. We will be devoting Chapter 3 to the Zigzag Path. You'll enjoy it. It's fun.

Before we close Chapter 2, we are going to look at the story of Cinderella and locate the structural components within it.

EXPLORATION OF CINDERELLA

Let's just recap the shape of a plot.

Beginning.

1. The story opens onto the protagonist's normal world but at a point of change.
2. A challenge or opportunity is presented which will bring about the start of change.
3. After tension inducing hesitation, the challenge or opportunity is accepted by the protagonist.

Middle
4. A rising arc of tension climbs to the 3 Cs and takes up approx. two thirds of the story in which obstacles are presented and overcome by the protagonist. In so doing, the protagonist develops inwardly.
5. The 3Cs. Crisis scene just before the Climax, during which the climax seems unobtainable. (2Cs only in a short story.)
6. Climax scene. Whew, it appears to have come good.
7. Crisis. Is all lost?
8. Confirmatory, or 'slipper test' as I call it, appears.

End

9. Resolution.
10. Conclusion – not always necessary these days.

This is the shape. Now let's track this shape within the story of Cinderella, and bring in the other components, much like mixing up that cake of ours.

CINDERELLA

The story of Cinderella has been around for 1000 years. Not just in Europe but throughout the world. Naturally enough, each version of the story took the cultural form of its region and religion.

Western Europe received Charles Perrault's version in 1760. He wrote it in France, at the court of Louis XV. This is the one in our national consciousness, whether it is in a book, film, or countless pantomimes, as I've already said. I'm not saying that Perrault established the structural form we use today, that was long before, in Greece. But I'm using this as most of you have seen the panto and will be familiar with the story.

We'll just remind ourselves of the basic plot before we set off.

Girl wants to go to the ball. Girl struggles to achieve her aim of going to the ball to show that she is loved and has resumed her rightful place. Girl achieves her aim of going to the ball which leads to her finding love, and status.

Cinderella

1. Cinderella, our protagonist, is in her **normal world**, skivvying in the kitchen with the servant, Buttons, (in the panto version). He is in **secondary character mentor** support. By his dialogue and behaviour Buttons **SHOWS** us who is the **protagonist**, and from the setting and discussion indicates Cinderella's situation. **The theme of injustice** is hinted at. (If you are not familiar with the panto version, you will find the story uses other mentors) Cinderella is the focus of attention as befits the protagonist. Though she is in her normal world at the beginning of the story, she MUST be at **point of change** to keep the attention of the audience.

2. And so she is. Almost immediately an **opportunity for change** arrives in the form of a ball invitation for the whole 'higher strata level' household. This household comprises her **antagonists** – the **secondary characters** -

her step-mother, and two step-sisters who live in luxury above stairs over-riding Cinderella's weak but well-meaning father. Cinderella is **motivated** at the point of change to go to the ball and sees her inclusion as a symbol of her return to her proper position as part of her family. It is a symbol of being loved again. Or at the very least she might meet someone who will love her.

3.   But, as is often the case, when an opportunity is presented, it takes a degree of nerve to 'go for it'. There is **tension** aplenty from the environment, characters, and inner person. This leads to 'Will she, won't she' accept the initial opportunity or challenge? Will she suggest that she is included? Will she pluck up that sort of courage? And who hasn't hesitated to accept such a potentially life changing opportunity, one that take us out of the comfort zone? With the support of her **mentor**, Buttons, she finally overcomes the tension inducing indecision and **accepts the challenge.** She begins her journey along the **rising arc of tension** away from the comfort zone, towards another world.

4.   The rising arc of tension is embarked upon when the **antagonists** (the 'steps') agree that she may come to the ball, on condition that she fulfils tasks they set. Her **antagonists**, put every obstacle in her way. Yes, she can go, if she finishes this, that and the other. She overcomes each **antagonistic** obstacle with the help of her **mentors**, and overcomes her inner **antagonistic** doubts, even though the ball keeps moving just out of her reach. Remember that mentors can change. At first it's Buttons, (in some versions) and the Fairy Godmother, and all sorts of little mice etc. With each betrayal of the promise made, each unfairness, we are SHOWN, through **exposition,** the theme – that of injustice. What a struggle, what **a rising arc of tension,** it's all designed to keep us hooked, to see the development of the character, and the unfolding of the plot. We readers can empathise because who hasn't felt the heavy hand of injustice at some stage of their life.

5.   We're now two thirds of the way through the book, at the point of the 3Cs. The first one is the **crisis scene.** The resolution of which will lead to the **climax scene**. It's the night of the ball, and here is Cinderella, all her tasks completed, her obstacles overcome, her part of the deal finally

completed. But... But... the final betrayal, the step-family reneges on the deal. **Oh the injustice**. By now we're well and truly relating to Cinderella. Her struggle is ours. She **must** win out, for **our** sakes. Cinderella is as self-sacrificing as ever and pretends to her father that it doesn't matter. She puts his well-being before hers. (This Cinderella is very wishy washy and compliant. A worthy heroine for the time in which it was written. Today we'd be tempted to slap her leg and tell her to get some backbone, but then I'm a cynical old bag). In the nick of time her **mentor**, in the shape of her Fairy Godmother, galvanises all the other mentors, **secondary** and **minor (mice etc)** into helping Cinderella achieve her aim, or motivation, of going to the ball. But she must be home by midnight. Whew. So are we in the clear? Is Cinderella home and dry? Is the story complete? Don't you believe it. Too easy by far.

6. The ball is the **climax scene, the 2nd C**. It's the **brightest** moment so far. Yes, she achieves her aim to take her rightful place alongside her peers, albeit anonymously. What's more, she finds love, in the shape of the Prince, even if she doesn't find it with her family. This will bring her to a far more elevated position. A-a-a-h, so she's won? Achieved her aim? Is the theme of injustice about to be addressed, and everything resolved? **Tension**, remember. Hold back as Perrault has done throughout. Don't let it come too easily. She's forgotten the deadline. Uh oh...

7. **Crisis, the 3rd C**. Ooops, apparent disaster. It is Cinderella's darkest moment. She flees as mid-night strikes. Everything seems lost, as though Cinderella, having struggled to reach the equivalent of Martin's escarpment, finds herself doomed to failure. She is stripped of her finery and reduced to her old clothes, her old role. But NO, she drops a slipper. (We'll ignore the perennial question of why the glass slipper didn't disappear along with all the other finery. We'd have sorted that out with some plausible reason, being the writers we are, but...) This disaster is a huge obstacle. Will it be overcome? Will Prince Charming find her? Will she be able to try on the slipper and prove that she is his lost love? Will she have developed and changed sufficiently to cross her **antagonists** one more time to achieve another **motivation**, a final **resolution** to the large problem that this story has been discussing? In other words, will injustice be overcome and love found - again? (Refer back to Martin. Having helped

his companion back up the escarpment, will he find a way over the unexpected obstacle of the river? If he perseveres, what a lot it shows about his character development and the growth of his self-esteem.)

8. **The confirmatory test, often known as the slipper test**. In Cinderella, it is Prince Charming who comes to find Cinders. Heroines today would do something 'active' about finding the slipper opportunity, rather than waiting, just as Martin has to find a solution to the river, which is his confirmatory test. Another solution would have been for a plane to have flown over the escarpment, and rescued them, but that's far too convenient and flat. No - the character has to drive onwards. In the pantomime it is not Cinderella driving forward, but Buttons sacrificing his own best interests - he's in love with Cinderella himself - and pushing Cinderella forward when the prince arrives with the slipper - a common mentor action. So Buttons helps her to achieve her aim, which has moved from going to the ball to achieving love with the Prince. Even though Cinders is pushed forward to try on the slipper, it is still up to her to insert her foot against pressure from the **antagonistic** 'Steps'. Will she won't she defy her step-mother and try the slipper on and therefore **confirm** her development?

9. **Resolution.** She tries on the slipper. It fits. Cinderella's truly loved by the Prince, and regains her place in society, and her father his place too. The **theme** has been addressed. Justice has been achieved, Cinderella's **motivation** also. The **protagonist** has developed. We as readers feel that in a way there is hope for our own battles. But, and here's another illustration of tension - what happens to the step-family? Are they punished? Thrown out? Wait for it. Keep the question unanswered, the tension going, the pages turned.

10. **Conclusion.** Cinderella is forgiving. She does not destroy her foes, as they attempted to destroy her. She's good. She's an example to us all. She forgives them and so all ends are tied.

Bear in mind that a conclusion is not necessary. Resolution in the form of a clear way forward is sufficient these days. I'm not going to pretend that Cinderella reflects contemporary attitudes. I will repeat that our golden girl is too passive. In this, Perrault was reflecting the society of the day. I use

Cinderella as an example because most of us are familiar with the story. I hope you can see that this common shape, with its common components allows us to access our readers' emotions without technical confusion.

If you're feeling worried, don't be. We're working together, remember, and rest assured that you really know all this. I'm just reminding you. The more you read and write, the clearer it will become.

Exercises. Read a short story and a novel. Note that the slipper test will be absent in the short story. Short stories are moments in time, and a confirmatory test isn't necessary. Pick out the points of shape, identifying mentors, antagonists, theme, motivation, and tension and SHOW.

Think of some points of change in your own life.

Look at some magazine pictures. Try and decide on the normal world of the main character in each picture and a point of change. Decide on the journey he/she is to undertake. Their motivation and theme.

Antagonist Exercises:

You need to get inside baddies, to sit in them, make them plausible and understandable. Few are psychotically evil. Many have become desperately competitive through jealousy, ambition, wrong upbringing, wrong ideology. We need to understand the antagonist, and perhaps even sympathise. How? Read widely about those who are bad. Remember your own falls from grace.

Write a rant against a particular event in the news. Try to reveal the source of the character's misguided beliefs within the monologue, and make the reader understand the speaker, or at least the speaker's belief in his views. Make sure that you choose a view with which you **disagree.**

Mentors: Who was a mentor when you were a child? Are they still in your life? Are they still in that role, or not? If not, why not? Have you ever mentored them? Are you mentoring them now? How does that feel for you both?

Chapter 3. The Zigzag Path

This is my secret weapon. It's fun too. First we need to talk about triggers for the imagination; the seeds from which can grow pretty big trees. Let's stay with Cinderella for a moment longer to consider the importance of 'character'.

The name, Cinderella, is a signal. We immediately picture a young girl in rags, and in her finery. We remember what happened to her within the concept of a self-indulgent family that excluded Cinderella. In other words, we are concerned with the character, and what happens to her.

Let's take another example. Imagine a headline stating that a radio station is launching an ageist policy. This is a concept. It's one we might ponder, but as fiction writers we'd know that we need a character to bring the concept alive.

Imagine that the headline said that *'Maria fell victim to ageist policy.'* Ah, we have our main character. We have someone we can stand alongside and with whom we can empathise. We have personalised the report.

Here's another. The concept is: *Plane Hijack foiled when hostages rescued.*

Personalise it. What about: *A lone hero rescues hostages of a plane hijack.* We're far more curious this time.

If you see a headline. *Woman destroys neighbour's Leylandii hedge* you'd picture the woman, and want to know more.

But hang on a moment, are headlines the only way to prod this wonderful imagination of yours? Where do ideas come from?

Try the following:

Dig about in your own past, your own inner obsessions. Take notice of pictures, photographs, features, newspaper items. Even a piece of music can trigger an idea, and inspire.

Then let your imagination take over and create a fictional protagonist within that scenario.

But how to make that character plausible and fully fleshed?

The Zigzag Path

Using the stream of consciousness Zigzag Path enables you to create a past, present and future for the protagonist. From that past will come the universal human emotional problem or experience (theme) that underpins his/her motivation. You conjure up secondary characters and minor characters, and much of the plot. You encourage exposition because you get inside your characters and really become them. You can see them, feel what they are feeling, use your senses as they need to be used, see their faces, body language, hear their voices, know all about them.

What's more, if you've been doing the Daily Pages you can do stream of consciousness. If you haven't, get going!

Let's take one of the ideas I've just mentioned.

Woman destroys neighbour's Leylandii hedge.

I find the idea triggers my imagination. I have a huge curiosity about why she would do this. Curiosity is a great asset for a writer. For me, it wouldn't be so intriguing if it were a man. Men have been known to take a saw to a hedge before, but Leylandii are big beasts, so a woman doing such a thing is more dramatic.

You will find that some subjects and headlines appeal to you, and others leave you cold. If you are to write from the heart, go with your instincts.

But on with the matter in hand.

Remember those questions you asked yourself in Chapter 1. Why, who, what, when, where, how? We're going to use them again. They're six of the most useful words in a writer's world.

Why would our protagonist do such a thing? What a product of huge anger - to destroy a neighbour's huge Leylandii hedge. Look at the headline again, and focus. Woman destroys neighbour's Leylandii hedge.

Have you an image? Can you see the woman? Can you see the hedge? Come with me while I work this out as though I am producing a plan for a novel. See the value of daily pages as I let my thoughts stream onto paper. Although I will use stream of consciousness I need to shape it, and focus on the protagonist primarily, since all things are relevant to her journey. I will need to keep reminding myself of this.

Let's go.

A grey haired woman springs to my mind, and a looming hedge. I see a vague neighbourhood of semi-detached 1930s houses. Sort of middle class, set today. So we have **who, where, when**. The woman isn't very elderly, but late middle aged.

She destroys her neighbour's Leylandii hedge. I can't picture the neighbour yet, so I'll leave him. Ah, at least I know I've chosen a him. But he isn't clear although we're at the start of knowing **who** he is. I'll make a note, put it in a box labelled neighbour. I know he'll be a secondary character since it's his hedge. It stands to reason he's important. So that will go on the label too. She will have her own box too, labelled protagonist. I could put it into a computer but I get ideas here there and everywhere, and like to write it down and have it in boxes. You put your ideas where you wish. Yes, I know I'm a Luddite, but it works for me.

Interestingly, if I had pictured the neighbour first, I might well have seen the story from his point of view, and made him the protagonist. My spark of interest is with the woman, so that's what will keep me interested.

My mind is running on a bit. This man will be the antagonist. Well, he has to be, hasn't he, if she cut down his hedge because I can see her doing it in anger. But let me argue that with myself. Perhaps the neighbour wanted it destroyed? But then it wouldn't have made headlines, and if he'd wanted it destroyed, he'd have worked on it with her, surely. Fine, so I'm sticking with anger and without his agreement. That's the way I'm going to play it. That conflict is begging to be explored, but not yet. I want to focus on the woman, and make progress with her.

What happened to drive her to it? **What** did he do? My mind's a blank, no creative imagination working on that yet. Leave it, and get back to **why**.

Why would she be driven to this act by the neighbour? Still nothing. This is too big a question at this stage. I have no idea, I would be guessing. It would lead me up a blind alley. I mustn't leap too far ahead and force it. I must relax, and enjoy this. I must be patient - writing isn't a race. I must just let my imagination crank up. Soon it will start to produce flickering scenes. Anyway, I've got more than I started with. I have two characters in embryo.

I'll go back to the hedge. I can see her carry the saw to the hedge. I can see her saw down all the Leylandii. Crash, bang, wallop. Ah, so I know **how** she did it –with a saw.

She didn't use the saw on anything else, not her own roses, not another neighbour's privet. She sawed down that Leylandii hedge. She was driven, or motivated, by the want to saw down that particular hedge. I can see that I'm making this headline come towards the end of the protagonist's journey. It's the climax of something.

Good, I've come up with motivation and something of the shape, and have the destruction scene in skeleton. There she is, sawing down old Stan's hedge. Ah, so I have a name for the neighbour. Trust your imagination to be working at the back of your head. It will do the work for you. We're another step forward. I'll make a note of that.

She wanted to remove that hedge. She wanted it so much that she'd risk punishment and censure.

Why?

But, hang on, I haven't yet thought of the name of the protagonist, I can see her but... No, I will have to wait for the name.

And here it is. It's just come to me. Audrey. I will call her Audrey. Why? Who knows? Maybe I knew an Audrey who looks like the character I can see.

Audrey takes a saw to the offending hedge. This story is becoming more personalised by the moment.

Perhaps the hedge was causing shade? Yes, my imagination is moving again. Is lack of shade enough of a reason to gain our sympathy for such an act of destruction?

No. The hedge has to keep the sun off something important.

Chrysanthemums spring to mind.

Yes, I could have her concerned about her chrysanthemums. But it's still not reason enough to gain our sympathy. It just leaves her as a vicious old bag.

You can see that my imagination is zigzagging between the past and the present. One question leads to another and then on into the future. Stream of consciousness exercises have helped to oil the wheels of creative imagining.

Suddenly I can see that Stan, the neighbour is jealous of her success with chrysanthemums, which were third in the competition last year. This year they are threatening to be even better.

But why would he mind, unless he was also growing chrysanthemums?

Yes, I'll have him second in last year's cup competition, and ripe to take first place this year as the usual cup winner has moved away. His only fear is that Audrey will snatch away his victory. So how can he stop this happening?

So, here we are, asking, how?

Things are rolling more smoothly now.

Later I will go into his past too, to see just why he is so competitive. In this way we can understand as well as dislike. It will create a more realistic story, and dialogue between the two. If you've kept up with the empathy exercises, the staying in the moment observations and the daily pages you can slide into your characters' bodies easily.

Back to Audrey. **Why** does she care so much for the blooms? What is my imagination going to come up with? This can take several days, or even weeks. I'm more used to it, so can hustle it all along for the sake of the chapter.

Suddenly I know she's only been in the neighbourhood for three years. She bought the house when she was made redundant from her secretarial position. So my imagination has come up with a stab at timetable and reason for being there.

So **why** did she start growing chrysanthemums? OK, let's go with where my imagination is taking me. Because... Stan tossed his weaker blooms into her garden, instead of composting them, slap bang on top of her head whilst she was weeding. Mmm, that shows us a lot about Stan. I can see the scene. They're on her hair, her back, falling to the ground. It's spring, the flower bed is friable, well looked after by Audrey, though this year she has only planted annuals. It is her first year at the house.

How rude of Stan.

Why didn't she object? Why didn't she call, 'Mr Bigalow, I think these belong to you.'? Why didn't she then toss them back over that Leylandii hedge which was just about ready for a trim but still a reasonable height?

Who knows, it might have landed right back on his bald bonce. Ah, so we now have a surname, and an image of the neighbour, and I can hear Audrey's voice. This guy is not nice, as well as bald.

So **why** didn't she give as good as she got? My imagination is straining at the leash to zigzag back into her past to find the answer.

What about her past?

If you're getting in a dither and thinking, I don't know where I am here, remember that you would be writing notes, keeping track. Here, we're just letting our creative imagination help us towards our goal – that of creating an accessible story. Just keep on reading this and you will get the general picture of my creative imagination working in a zigzag pattern solving problems for me. When you come to do it for yourself, you will use your imagination in this way, or adapt it to your own preference, but you will have seen how you can trust your mind to help you, once you've trained it to stream around an idea.

Back to the matter in hand. I'm going back into her past. I'm picturing Audrey as she was in her early 30s. She is still single, but with a boyfriend, a new one. Her only sister is married with children, her name is Margery and she is older. Their father has had a stroke, all her life the mother has made a virtue of being helpless. The sister and mother designate Audrey as the one who should live at home and care for her father, and for mother too, who is a manipulator and weeps if voices were ever raised in anger. Let me just say here, that don't worry about tenses and spelling. Just let it all stream out, just as I am doing.

Audrey complied. It's what she did - comply. She was conditioned from an early age to do so. **Why?** She knew her place. Her sister was the clever one, the prettier one. Audrey's had been a difficult birth. Her mother's 'ill health' had begun then, as she never failed to remind Audrey, creating an implicit obligation.

You see, you have to find plausible reasons for people's behaviour, so you, as the writer, can understand completely where they are 'coming from'.

Audrey accepted her responsibilities, though scared of losing her boyfriend, Michael, because she could not articulate her needs in the face of her mother's emotional blackmail and her sister's reminder of her duty.

Once, Audrey protested, but to no avail. *'You should have found a husband earlier,'* the sister had said. *'It's all a matter of timing. Who knows if Michael is the one anyway? If he sticks around, then he's right for you and if he bolts, then you should be grateful to us for bringing it to a head. And remember poor mother's health, never a day without aches and pains since you were born.'* Ah, I've got Margery's voice, and tightly permed hair in that flash of a 'backstory' scene. For this is what's called the backstory; this fleshing out of the past.

Audrey had realised the truth of her sister's words. It was her duty to put herself last. Michael had not hung about to see if she would ever be free, and neither was he about to marry and move in with her parents. Audrey felt it was her fault, she hadn't proved desirable enough to overcome her parent's rudeness to Michael. When her father died she had resumed her secretarial work to help keep her mother in the way she deserved, or so it was implied. Four years ago Audrey had been made redundant.

You see, here I've altered things a bit, as my thought processes have refined things. Earlier I said she had been made redundant three years ago, and had bought the house. However, my imagination has ferreted around and come up with details of the family, and I have to eliminate the mother, to make her alone. An extra year would be good. Remember that I did this with Martin, and introduced an antagonist for the journey?

You might be able to see that I'm drawing in reasons for her anger, an anger that has been repressed and only bursts into action over the hedge. Once I've done all this, I'll decide where to actually start the story, and how much of this backstory will be interwoven, very lightly. I'm making notes all the time. I'm getting inside my character, knowing her past and present, her voice, her looks, her mannerisms. She's becoming fully fleshed, and I've done it without sitting down and working out a list. A lot of it comes when driving a car, or standing in a supermarket queue, or something like that. I'm also getting ideas about the setting, the timing, the antagonists (no mentors yet)

So, she was made redundant, four years ago. **Why?** The other secretary had been there just one year longer, though she had done very little work in comparison. Though hurt and resentful, Audrey hadn't objected. After all, rules were rules, and if they'd wanted her that much, they'd have kept her. It was her fault, again.

Then her mother died. That's why I shifted the chronology. I had to fit in the mother dying. It is then that Audrey discovers that the family house, which she assumed would be hers after all these long years of duty, was to be divided between Audrey and her sister. This meant it had to be sold because Audrey could not afford to buy out Margery.

Good, now I'm working out why she's in the Leylandii house.

So, here she was, being manipulated again. But she accepted it, because it made sense. How could she object?

The backstory has stalled for a moment, so back to the hedge, and the chrysanthemums. Let's prime the pump. Why were the chrysanthemums so important? Did she like flowers?

In this small house she wanted to create a wonderful garden, one like the one she had worked so hard to create at her parents' home. Then, it had kept her sane to nurture the plants, pouring her love into them. Then she had to walk away from her creation, from plants she had raised from seed, from her child substitutes, almost.

Got it. By taking another tack, I've also come up with backstory as well as matters pertinent to the hedge.

So, when Stan had flung over the plants, she did not object, because she never had. Instead, she swallowed the bullying, for that's what it was. Bullying she had been suffering all these years. That and imposed guilt over being the root of her mother's supposed ill health. This could have led to a lack of self-esteem. Basically we're talking injustice here, aren't we? So, here's the **theme**. (I've chosen this again as it might help you to have a similar theme to Cinderella, and perhaps to some extent, Martin's story) So she swallowed her indignation and brushed the earth out of her hair, and instead of complaining, she planted Stan's rejected plants. They prospered. She had her creations again, the babies that had been denied to her. Ah. Got it again.

For their sake, she listened to Stan as he boasted on and on about his own chrysanthemums and used his tips which he was unwittingly giving her in the year following his disposal of his rejects all over her head.

She never mentioned that she was growing his cast-offs. She never invited confidences, because she didn't think anyone would be interested in anything she had to say.

As always, the previous year all the neighbours entered the town flower show in whatever category they chose. Several chose chrysanthemums.

I have to think of timing here. Let's have Audrey entering her chrysanthemums too. She does it to fit in with the street. Her babies, so carefully nurtured, gained third place. She was totally thrilled, for them, and a bit for herself, though she'd been brought up to think that self-appreciation was next to the devil! This worm needs to turn. I can see why she is as she is, I can understand, and I like her, but I want her to have a goal, I want her to address the theme. Membership of the Chrysanthemum Club is part of the prize.

Stanley was furious.

Right. So I'm working towards the importance of the chrysanthemums in that they were a **symbol** of all that she had not had. They were the children she had been denied. She had made them flourish as the garden at her parents' home had flourished until she had to sell it. She wanted her chrysanthemums to take their rightful place, she wanted to succeed in something, just for once. She wanted to be second to Stan's first prize in the next competition.

But then she sees the shade that the unclipped Leylandii hedge is producing, shade that threatens to cast gloom over ALL her garden. She is worried. Stan has not trimmed the hedge that autumn, following the show. Even worse, she sees him putting what she thinks is fertilizer at the base.

When she asks him about his hedge cutting plans he tells her he is going to cut it in the spring.

Spring has come and nothing happens to the hedge, except that it grows more and more. The shade is all over the tiny narrow garden. Worse, she sees him putting more fertilizer at the base.

Her motivation is firming. She wants to protect her plants and secure their second place prize winning position. She does not want anything to be cavalierly taken from her. So, I've unearthed her **motivation**, and am reinforcing the theme.

Each day Audrey waited and watched, seeing her blooms struggling, her tiny garden dark and dingy, until she had decided that something must be done. And the only one who could do it, and protect her 'babies' was her. Soon they would wither and die. For once she must take a stand.

I've led myself into the plot here, I think, so I'll run with it. I need to know more about Stan and summon up a mentor for Audrey, but that can wait. Let's go with what's coming into my mind. I've zigzagged into a starting point I could have her in her normal world, looking at the hedge, and worrying, talking to her plants, knowing it is almost too late - they are dying. Then have her going round to reason with Stanley, saying that she only wanted to come second to him. Could this be the point of change? Remember, I'm putting all of this into the relevant boxes and will thereby arrive at a point where I can organise the story. At that stage I will decide how much of her past to convey, and indeed, how to convey it.

Let's go on with the Zizagging.

She'd be nervous. She starts to walk round to his front door, but her courage fails her. I can see her; she's smartened herself up, put on her Church shoes, and her earrings, gold with small sapphires, a present from Michael, and precious to her. She feels more courageous now. At the front door she feels ridiculous at the thought of making a fuss, and sure that somehow she's brought this situation about. What if he shouts at her? She shows this by stepping back off the porch, smoothing her hair, touching an earring. She reaches across the step and gives the bell a quick push. There's no response. No sound inside.

She scuttles home, relieved not to have spoken to him. This hesitation over taking the first step away from her normal world would raise the tension. It would SHOW her as she is; timid, self doubting.

Yes, I'm really thinking seriously about this as the start of the story; her normal world and the start of the point of change.

But how I am going to make her take that second step, of accepting the challenge, of reaching and moving past the point of change? Let's try having her retreating to the kitchen, making a cup of tea, looking out through the window and seeing again the failing blooms, in the shade of the big hedge. Perhaps she could catch sight of a photograph of her sister's children. Her own arms feel empty. We could perhaps hear in her mind her sister's words about timing, and relationships and interweave that part of her backstory. A chance for a bit of interior monologue here.

On second thoughts, I'm going to open the story in the kitchen, with her looking at the plants, I'm not going to have her going round to his door previously, and I'm not going to mention her wanting an improved place in the competition yet. I'm going to hold back. All we know at the moment is her care for her plants.

She looks at her tea cup, her solitary tea cup. She looks at the chrysanthemums again and finally grasps the nettle.

She knows he's out, but will go round when he's in. She hears his car returning, and puts on her church shoes, and her best earrings to give her courage. She'll ask nicely but firmly. Surely he can't still be in a mood after last year's Chrysanthemum Cup Competition? She's petrified as she leaves her house but this time Stanley is passing, going to post a letter. She tries nice, explaining that his hedge is killing her Chrysanthemums. He says he'll try and get round to trimming the hedge.

She asks when? He says that it might be that evening, but not to worry her pretty little head, they're only plants, after all. He struts off. She feels sick because she knows, or fears, he won't. Yes, that's a good scene, it will work well, and introduce the protagonist and antagonist, and hint at the theme of injustice. We've seen his arrogance, her request for her right to light, and the tension of not knowing if he'll trim it this evening.

So, we're at the start of the point of change. Will he won't he trim the hedge? She wonders if she should have made more of a fuss. Should she go and do so now? No, she'll wait to see what happens. She doesn't want a scene. That's the hesitation. Good, what now?

At that point, her friend, a retired solicitor who is also a member of the Chrysanthemum Club drives along, on his way home from a meeting. Excellent. If I'd had the confrontation in the porch of Stanley's house, I couldn't have had this introduction to a mentor type character. Neither could I have had another dialogue which I'll need, because I've decided that at this stage I can SHOW through the conversation a little more about the situation. In other words, I'm introducing the competition, extending the reader's understanding of the situation, as well as making them wonder if there could be a relationship here, or at least the hope of one. Tension, tension.

John stops. He gets out of the car and walks round, they don't stand too close. Good, I've a name for him. A strong name. He asks how she is, how the hedge situation is going, there's so little time if she's to get the plants ready for the competition. How unreasonable it is that Stan didn't trim it in the autumn as usual. Surely he can't be that small minded as to fear she'll improve on her third place? She could say that all she could hope for was second, so she was no threat to his position as potential champion. And anyway, it was the health of her plants she was really worried about. She could say something about it being such a shame that Alfred moved, he was such a lovely man and really deserved the Club Championship last year.

So this knowledge is now in the hands of the reader.

Audrey is so grateful to hear a friendly voice and even more so when John offers to help, reaching out and touching her arm. It's the first time she's been touched by anyone for years.

She is reinforced, somehow, as she turns to go inside. He also says, 'But maybe it's too late already. Can the plants survive at this late stage? Maybe it would be better just to give up?' He doesn't like to see her worried like this. Or some such. Then he drives off. She watches him. So, she has a reason to give up, and a reason to go on. Which will it be? Suddenly we see some steel – perhaps as a result of his touch on her arm, the look in his eye - as she calls after him, though he can't hear, that if Stan wants a battle, then he'll get one. Her rage takes her by surprise.

Ah, so suddenly this is a battle. Yes, that would make a satisfactory scene, and move us onwards in the point of change.

She has all evening to pace about as nothing happens to the hedge. We are into the deadline tension trick - now or never. She stares at the photographs on her mantelpiece of her ex-boy friend, the photographs of the old house, or herself as a child with her life in front of her. What life? She removes her earrings, throws them in the bin. How ridiculous to hold onto the past like this. A **symbolic** act. I'm staying in the moment in all these scenes, making notes as I go, putting them into the PLOT box.

She pours sherry for herself. Her mother had said nice women never drank alone. She almost pours it back, then sips it. It is another obstacle overcome, another symbolic statement, another move onwards through the point of change. She downs it in a gulp, checks the hedge. Nothing has happened. She goes to bed.

I'm not sure what she's going to do. Neither will I let the reader know because it will leave it on a hook. They'll want to read on to find out what happens.

I think this will end up being a novel, I'm thinking in chapters, and it could run to the 3cs with the taking down of the hedge as the climax. There'd be repercussions after the climax at the 2/3 top of the arc of tension, creating the third C, a crisis. Perhaps Stan calls the police – well of course, because of the headline. My word, what a 'do' that would be. It would bring in Margery, appalled at the public humiliation. John would put up bail and act for her. Perhaps the street would appear on her behalf, perhaps she'd become a heroine... The court case would definitely make a slipper test.

Also, it would be good to have a sub-plot led by Stan, to see his side of it, and his counter actions to her actions. That would be required if it's a novel. If it's a short story, it would end at the taking down of the hedge, and the approval of the neighbours, who would see off Stan. We're coming to sub-plot and short story, don't worry.

Back to the Zigzagging. Where am I going now? In the morning she looks out of her bedroom window, staring at her poor struggling blooms. She looks around at the other houses, the other gardens – this will enlarge our understanding of her setting.

Suddenly she is charged with determination. She must stand firm, just for once. She will face him again and… what? She has to think of something.

The mentor phones. She answers on the bedroom phone, in her nightie. It makes her feel bold, somehow. He suggests she could transplant the fledgling plants to a bed in his garden, because the only other answer is to take Stanley and his hedge to court if he won't address the issue.

Ah, a choice to be made. She's been offered an escape by the mentor yet again, but also a way forward. There's also a bit of a sense of romance coming here.

The offer of a flower bed is tempting, it would solve one problem, and lead to potential happiness, but then Stan would have won, and she would have given way, again. Which is she to choose? So we have another bit of tension. Can you see how easily your imagination helps you, and brings you presents like this?

She dresses, not in smart clothes, but her working clothes. She is beginning to start to be the person that she could always have been. The reader sees this. She knocks on his door and threatens court action.

He mocks her with the comment that the plants will have withered away before the case reaches court. He taunts her with the words 'It's all a matter of timing.'

Ah, now my imagination has married her sister's remark with Stan's, all of which is tucked in the information boxes. So somehow I must bring in the importance of this remark either now, or before this moment, or after, as I interweave that bit of her past. Let's see what we can do with it.

Something clicks in Audrey. She could be standing on the porch step, and seeing Margery's face saying those same words. They were part of the interior monologue in the kitchen, if you remember. Trust your unconscious, it will throw up something like this moment. Then Sidney barks. 'Did you hear me?'

Audrey is back in the here and now, on the front step. Yes, this is the point of change, she is about to embark on the rising arc of tension, on her motivated journey towards her goal, to address the theme of injustice. The hedge must come down.

Bad move, Stanley. She returns to the house. The mentor phones again. She asks if he will represent her. He offers to do it free. She is proud and won't hear of that. She asks him about the time it would take.

Indeed, they would run out of time.

Ah, so what now? She has to decide how to cut down the hedge. With its downfall, would tumble all the past injustices in her life.

How she does it I would sort out with more of the same, but I won't bore you. I'm sure you have the idea, and just look at the progress we have made. By the mere act of letting stream of consciousness take over as we focussed on the image of a woman destroying her neighbour's hedge, a great deal has been achieved, and more of the same will bring the whole story to your door.

To recap:

I've looked backwards and forwards and provided a logical sequence of events that have driven Audrey to today's action. I've also revealed the underpinning emotion, the universal human experience, or the theme on which the story rests.

The theme is injustice due to her low self-esteem.

The hedge and Stan have become the symbol of all that has obstructed her all her life, all that has been taken from her, all the injustices of her life. By striking back, she can rectify the imbalance of power. She can resolve the injustice of the situation. Please be aware that frequently the protagonist's aim encapsulates in a symbolic sense all that he/she hopes to achieve. We will be looking at symbolism later.

Basically I feel I know Audrey by now, and can understand her motivation. I can also imagine how she feels. I know Stan, and can imagine the person he is.

At this point I would get inside the character of Stan rather more, and John, using the same method, though a great deal will flow from continued work on the plotting, which we're embarking on next.

What I try to remind myself is to argue with myself, and my imagination. I must make sure that the actions, and reactions are plausible. I have to remember that my reader must be able to identify with our protagonist's struggle.

Remember also how we delved into Audrey's back story to pin down her motivation: The realised need to allow sunlight to her plants, the unrealised need to address the injustice in her life.

Exercises

Work with one of these sentences to produce a story, using the zigzag method.

The secret was all she had that was hers.
The man was too tall, but would have to do.

Chapter 4 Exercises and notes designed to reinforce understanding of the structural components

Motivation Exercise.

1. Take yourself for a walk. As you pass real-life characters ask yourself why they are doing a particular thing. If you pass a house, ask yourself why someone chose that house. Why paint it that colour? Why plant that tree? What is the aim, the motivation? I-m-a-g-i-n-e something interesting, something with dramatic potential.

2. Read the newspaper. Ask why someone did what they did, said what they said. Summon up the reason. Ask this every time an event puzzles you. From now on that little three letter word - why - must be at the forefront of your mind. Why? Why? Why? Remember your children tugging at your trousers, or skirt? *'Why, Mum?' 'Why, Dad?'* Remember yourself doing it. Go on, it's easy to get back into that past where images have a brightness denied to us in the adult world.

Why would Mary Bloggs hold a firework party in June?

Why would Jo from down the road leave her family?

Why are your neighbours celebrating their sixth wedding anniversary with such gusto?

Remember that curiosity creates writers.

Protagonists/main characters.

Let's look at a few tips to reinforce the Zigzag Path, allowing it to help you create totally believable protagonists, with whom both the reader and writer can identify.

As we know, there is usually only one protagonist in a piece of fiction. One who'll drive the plot, one who is motivated to 'chop down the Leylandii' or 'rescue the hostages'.

We gave Audrey a name.

Why?

As I've already suggested, it personalises a character. It helps the writer identify with their creation.

I find that I have names that I associate with friends - positive names. I have others that I associate with non-friends, and there are those that I've observed in use. Some are cosy, some are not. I distribute them carefully, using the 'nice' names for my main characters, and dumping the 'nasty' on those with the darker edge. Apart from a bit of retribution (yes, I am a toad) it helps me focus the correct emotion on the appropriate character.

Exercise

Take two names that mean the following for you. Nice and nasty. Write a page on each. Why you like the name and the person who 'owns' it, why you don't. Then destroy it. It's safer that way. Then use these names in a scene. Have the nice name entering a café and seeing that there is one chair left. Be that nice person. Be in his or her skin. See the room as she sees it. The nice name heads towards the one vacant seat remaining at a table for two.

Another person enters behind her. They are the nasty and rush to overtake. They arrive at the table together. Who takes possession of the only chair? What does the nice name do?

What does he/she really feel?

Have the same scenario, but with you in the body of the nasty person entering the café behind the nice. What happens? How does the nasty name behave? Be that nasty person. How can you slip in some reason for their nastiness? Is there any guilt once they hog the chair? Is there any condemnation from the person already at the table, or a waitress? How does this alter, or not, the nice person's behaviour at that moment?

You could also consider taking over the body of the person sitting at the table. That person would be aware of the situation, as both approach. What is that person sitting at the table feeling? Perhaps they're dreading having to share the table. Why are they alone in the first place? What does the fracas provoke in the person already sitting at the table? Does the fracas symbolise something in their life? Be aware that getting inside each body gives a whole new perspective on the scene. In other words, altering the protagonist changes the story fundamentally.

When considering names I also pay attention to the period. If it is set in the past, I choose an appropriate name. Names reflect age, fashion, class.

Nicknames reflect personality, and can reflect a development within your character - during the course of your story your character might out grow their nickname. Nicknames can also be an example of abuse of power - perhaps someone knowingly insists on calling your character by a nickname they've long hated.

Exercise

Think of a male character who is about to set sail from Bristol to seek his fortune in 1900. What's an appropriate name?

What if it was a female character? What's her name? Match the names to class and profession.

You don't know what name's appropriate? Nip out to the library and have a quick skim through autobiographies, biographies, novels set in that period and deduce. Ask the librarian for help. Or use the internet. Writers have to research all the time, as they are more often than not writing outside their immediate experience or/and knowledge.

I think of my character's age, habits, mannerisms. I remember that these can change as the story progresses to show the character's development.

For instance, as Audrey arrives at the stage in her life when she embarks on the destruction of the Leylandii, she will have embarked on a personality change too. She will be 'striking back'. She will be determined, if still rather frightened. She will have come to a decision, though doubts might intrude. Her body language will change to reflect this, as will her bearing and her mannerisms. So too, will Martin outgrow his body language.

If you don't understand about body language, read it up in a book.

Exercise

Find some magazine pictures of three different people.

Think of some mannerisms that could reflect nervousness in these characters. Now, find another three, and impose on them a hard emotional shell, but a soft centre. How could you reveal this? You might like to consider that perhaps someone would stroke a cat. Perhaps a toughie would help an old lady across the road. (We'd just have to hope she wanted to cross in the first place) Perhaps someone else would release a butterfly trapped behind glass.

Check the mannerisms appropriate to another age, another religion, another country. Perhaps use the Internet. I mention again a trip to the library. Use it, or lose it. Libraries are essential to our well-being. We are privileged to have such a service. Librarians like to help. Writing is solitary, so work with others when you can.

Here's another task. Create some mannerisms appropriate to a future age – this is a chance for your creative imagination to kick up a storm.

Let's go on to clothing.

How do your characters dress in a past, present or future age? Their clothes should reflect who they are. It would also dictate how they move. Imagine walking in a crinoline.

If, for instance, a character dresses casually it could indicate self-confidence, or a rebellious nature. Be sure you have decided which. If a woman wears a twin set, is that through choice, or habit, or convention? Does she dress to please her man? You must know.

If she dresses to please convention or someone else, might she change her style as indicative of her development as the story progresses? What hairstyle does she have? If someone is heartbroken they often cut their hair short, with an almost savage look resulting. If you discover during the Zigzag Path that heartbreak is on the cards, and actually happens, then create a scene in which the hair is hacked short. But remember to have it longer to begin with. You can always go back and alter things, remember, right up to the last minute. Nothing's set in stone with writing.

If it is a future age, how is the character's position in the hierarchy indicated? What about the character in the past age?

We mentioned Audrey's change of dress between her attempts to talk to Stan the first time, and then the next day. How do you think she dresses as she embarks on the destruction of the hedge? Does she wear gloves, which she rips off as she gets hotter and dirtier? Perhaps she tears a nail, and gets dirt beneath them. She could hear her mother's critical voice. '*A lady should always wear Marigolds, Audrey.*' It simply adds energy to her activities. When finished, would she be more comfortable to be the new Audrey, or hanker for the old?

What about our Martin's clothes? How would they alter as his day progresses?

Consider this sentence.

Brian sat quite still, listening.

For your information, Brian is sitting in a room. Create a very quick character sketch of no more than a page. Your imagination might be influenced by having known a particular Brian. I like to think that by now you are creating scenes quite naturally, that you are staying in the moment and **showing** this. That you are including the sounds he is hearing. Perhaps the chair digs into the back of his legs, or whatever **you** would feel if you were Brian.

Ask yourself: Why is he listening? Why is he sitting quite still? What sort of chair is he sitting on? Where is the room, where is the chair? Is he in danger? Is he upset? Who is he? How is he sitting? Is he tense or eager? And so on.

If you are working in a group, you will find you all have your own interpretation of each of these exercises, because your unique voices are being honed as we go through the handbook. You are delving into your experiences, your imagination and your emotions. You are creating original work that is vibrant and alive.

A general character exercise

There are three deck chairs. Someone is sitting on one of them. Which one? How does it feel? What is the weather doing? Who's the person? What are they doing there? If they are meeting someone, who? Fill all three deck chairs. Maybe there's a child. Do her/his legs reach the pebbles? Do the chairs shift on the pebbles? Be there. Ask all the questions necessary to explore motivation, theme, plot and the backstory through use of the Zigzag Path. You will find that it's becoming a quicker and quicker method for you.

Secondary characters

Secondary characters are of less importance than the main character or protagonist as we know, but of greater importance than the 'walk-on' parts. They are there as foils to the protagonist. They can be mentors. They can be antagonists. Whatever they are, they are an intimate part of the story, an essential device to create tension, plot and character development. Think of the films you've seen, and the books you've read. Kevin Costner is the protagonist in The Bodyguard, with Whitney Houston as the character of secondary importance. It is Kevin who is motivated, who has the inner and outer problem to solve - to save Whitney/to allow himself to feel emotion. He has clamped down on these after his emotions got the better of him in a previous case, and he forgot his professionalism.

Whitney is a secondary character, and so too her son, and the young driver who gets roped in - as a sort of mentor to Kevin. You can sort out the rest after you've watched the film. Or maybe you disagree with me? That's fine. It is because we all come from different experiences that we perceive books, films, plays and indeed life, from our own standpoint.

Choose those characters which are secondary for you. Don't forget the antagonists.

Think of Audrey, the Leylandii woman. Stan is involved, but it is 'our' Audrey who is intent on destroying the hedge. Audrey is the one who is motivated. She has the reason to destroy it. It is her motivation or want that will drive the story. It is her backstory that will give us the theme. If you have a different perception to me, you may well have made Stan the injured party and protagonist, and Audrey a walloping nutter and secondary character. It's up to you.

The Fairy Godmother and Buttons are secondary characters in Cinderella.

So is her father, and the step-family. The father doesn't really take a mentor or antagonist role, he is benign but weak and almost in need of Cinderella's protection. The 'steps' as we know take the antagonist role. Are there any other mentors or antagonists? This isn't a test. I just wonder what your opinion is. Maybe if you think back to the panto you've seen you might consider the Prince and his entourage.

As we realised when using the Zigzag Path for Audrey's story, the secondary characters need to be fleshed out along the same lines as the main character. Though we didn't do it, you know how to use the method.

As writers we need to know the secondary characters intimately. We must know their intent, their reasons for doing what they are doing, their motivation. We must know the reason for their existence in our piece of fiction. Do remember that you don't introduce a character, and then just let them disappear. If they were there in the first place, they must have been fulfilling a need for us as the writer. Therefore, they must be **plausibly** exited off into the wings.

Minor characters

Minor characters need not be drawn in anything like the same detail as your main character. Their function is to A) interact with the main and secondary characters and/or B) to help the writer provide the reader with necessary information and /or C) to move the story along.

They must always be integral to the plot. If you can do without them, then do so.

Exercise

Refer back to Brian. There he is, in the room you have created, sitting on the chair you have provided. Have a minor character entering. Whoever it is they must fulfil their function - to provide necessary information, to reveal something of the person, to move the story along. Perhaps it is a secretary to inform him that he has an appointment at 2 p.m. Be precise. Don't have a blanket term such as 'this afternoon'. Precise statements focus the mind of the reader. You must stay in Brian's body. You must see this messenger, not be in the messenger's body. This is called staying in Brian's point of view, and we'll come to that soon.

Perhaps this is an appointment Brian is dreading. How can you show this without a tedious explanation?

Remember mannerisms, perhaps he pulls his tie away from his neck. Perhaps he could snap at her, something he only ever does under pressure. Surely he would cancel it if he's listening for something? You know what that something is, so whatever happens here, the minor character action must inform, and move the story forward.

Theme

Let's have a quick recap of theme. I feel that the theme is something that comes naturally out of the character exploration during the Zigzag Path. You know by now that this deeper universal experience or problem is essential, that it is different from motivation. You know that it can be one of many things; revenge, injustice, coming to terms with the past, anger, betrayal, redemption... Most authors write out of the same theme again and again. It is what comes out of their own experience.

Plot

I think we've done enough on the plot/vehicle/shape. If I mention it again, you'll scream.

Tension

I think that you are aware of tension, of the obstacle/solution situation that is necessary, whether it be an overt tension, like the scaling of an escarpment, or a covert tension, like waiting for a phone call, and when it the phone rings how do we crank the tension? Try - it is not the person your character is expecting, but an innocuous caller. How does your character get rid of them to leave the line free? Once she does, how does she show her tension as the clock ticks round? When it finally rings, and it is the expected call you'd need a few false starts. Perhaps the first thing the caller discusses is the weather. How is our character going to bring the conversation round to the real nitty gritty?

Exposition is the creating of scenes. Well, haven't you been doing that? But we will be working in more depth on the components of exposition very shortly.

Unique Voice: Continue with the daily pages and stay in the moment for every day activities once a day.

Now we are moving to the **short story**.

Chapter 5. Short Story

The novel is said to be fiction at its highest state of development. To grasp all that it entails is to grasp the essentials of writing fiction. So what is the short story? A compressed novel?

No, the short story is a distinct form. So how does it differ? What special adaptations does it call for?

What it is **not** is a précis of a novel, or a summary. A story must have the same structural components as a novel or play, or screen play, though with 2Cs, not three. It does not have a Slipper Test as a rule. A short story should explore a single idea, make a single point, close with a single denouement, creating a single effect.

Whereas, as we have seen, a novel works in a more generalised atmosphere, with several strands carrying the story forward, headed always by the protagonist, of course.

What do I mean by several strands? Secondary characters, all with their own lives, help to progress the novel. Some of the characters have a sub-plot (Learn more about the sub-plot in the next chapter). Even those without sub-plots have a past and future, and a general life flow interwoven with that of the protagonist.

A short story is a piece of creatively imagined life taken **out** of the flow of that life. This moment taken out of the flow is an acute problem, not the prolonged chronic problem of the novel.

Though I've just said that the short story is a moment taken out of a life, it needs to be clear how this moment fits into the life as a whole. Therefore the story should imply a before and after, and a context.

Be aware that your short story should have resonance with the reader, a reminder of a broader reality.

A short story must have a beginning, middle and end, be unified and neatly packaged. It is a helpful idea to keep in mind the three unities of Greek drama, which has the same tight structural requirements of the modern short story.

1   **Unity of time** – a short story usually covers a mere 24 hours.
2   **Unity of place** – a short story often starts and finishes in the same place. Not always, by any means, but often.
3   **Unity of action** - the story is told from only one viewpoint.

The Plot or story line: If you are writing a genre short story (a story for a particular market - often a women's magazine) much is dependent on the plot because of the nature of that genre market. Editors want something they can take in quickly, something that will please their readers, something that the readers expect. It could be a surprise twist. It might need a crime/resolution plot, or simply a chronological outcome. Whatever it is, it will need to be clear cut. If it is a literary short story (one not written for a particular market) it can be free of restraint.

Whatever type of short story you are writing, you must bear in mind that because it is such a tight discipline, with a singleness missing in the novel, it might be a good idea to plan it precisely before embarking on the writing. Sit back, let the idea turn over, make sure you have your outcome, picture the situation, know the build up to the opening of the story (the back story) using the Zigzag Path. Know the characters, especially the protagonist. Know the setting. Then outline the story. But if you prefer not to plan, then that's fine. It's your choice, you're in control.

The setting is often of great importance in a short story. It is often the reason the character has the single problem to resolve. Perhaps a setting reminds the protagonist of a past issue which can no longer remain unresolved. Perhaps the protagonist is caught in a trap, a release from which will not only resolve the situation, but also hint at a broader reality.

You will need the normal world, the point of change, the rising arc of tension scenes/events rising to the 2CS. There is probably not a confirmatory test, because of the nature of the discipline, but again this is dependent on the requirements of your market. Then there is the clear-cut outcome or resolution, or perhaps merely a confirmation of the way in which the character has changed – or not.

There is not time to make characters complex, not time to show them developing beyond that acute moment of time though there can be future resonance.

The opening must convey information. The reader should be given answers to a few basic questions. What? Where? When? This must be conveyed in enough detail to get their bearings, but with a light enough hand so that the reader isn't bored into putting it down. There's a need for some hint of the main situation. Remember you have the course of the story in which to reveal whatever else is necessary, such as why, how, who.

Having established your situation and characters you'll need to take them through a series of scenes to reveal them more fully and develop, or disclose, the conflict you've set up.

The story must move. You can't afford to linger over descriptions or reflection that doesn't progress the protagonist. Tell it through action and dialogue.

For instance: If it's vital that Tony has a blue van, then say Tony's blue van roared round the corner, rather than Tony had a blue van and she saw it roaring round the corner. Double or treble things up into layers as much as possible to keep up the pace, much as we saw in Martin's interior bus scene.

Remember tension. It may be acute, or subtle. But either way, you know by now that the reader expects something interesting to happen much of the time, though they're unable to guess what.

The climax is more precise than in a novel. We know it when it happens. It can take the form of a revelation, or can be punchy, or a twist.

It can end on this note of climax, the second of the Cs or resolution.

The resolution can be something unrevealed. Perhaps a question from a stunningly boring spouse. *'What are you doing with that bread knife, my dear?'*

Whatever it is, the resolution is best kept brief, or the impetus is lost and the pace becomes contrived.

Whatever else it is, the last lines shouldn't whitter on, trailing off into an anti-climax but they must be functional.

When revising: Study the story's construction. Is the shape sound? Have you built up the rising arc of tension? Have you given information without stopping the pace? Does it start in the normal world, at a point of change? Is it plausible? Can you accept the characters?

Frequently interior monologue or dialogue is used to draw into the present some incidents of the past, or flashbacks. We'll look at flashbacks in Chapter 7.

Be aware that if you're writing short stories for magazines, you should analyse their requirements carefully. See my notes on analysis which follow. Some magazines have guidance notes on their requirements, and these are available from their editorial offices and sometimes online.

Example

If I was to create a short story involving Martin, I'd take a facet of the concept and contain it within a brief moment in time while addressing the same theme.

Here goes, and I make no apologies for re-inventing the plot. It's the only way I could think of to make it work, but you might well come up with something better.

I'll start with changing the setting. The desert road is too much a flow of a life situation. I'll have him in his normal world and attitudes - at the base camp, having committed another misdemeanour, one that has resulted in detention, and the decision to send him home. Martin's straight into his point of change, and intent on running away, anything rather than go back to the city and his brother. To aid his escape he's stolen food and money.

Henry tries to stop him, by saying how much he'd miss him, how he is one of the best in the class, if only he'd let others see it. How if he runs away he'll jeopardise the future of the summer camps (obstacle/tension) Martin goes anyway. *'I'll never be accepted now and what do I care what happens? Everyone thinks I'm just a loser so why prove them wrong.'* Then he heads up the escarpment behind the base camp, in the dark. So, we've seen his normal world (or normal behaviour), then the point of change. So the theme is selfishness caused by low self-esteem. His motivation is to avoid going home, by running away.

He sets off up the escarpment, overcoming all sorts of problems, (antagonists) still thinking of how Henry had said he is one of the best in the class, if only he'd let others see it (mentor). He thinks of his mother, who had said the same thing before she died. He thinks of his brother, who is always in trouble for theft, but perhaps that's where his new trainers came from. Was his brother doing it for him, so he could come on this trip? He convinces himself that his brother wouldn't do something like that for him, because he's always calling Martin a wimp.

Just as he's about to reach the top, he becomes aware of someone halfway up the escarpment, calling out to him. It's Henry, who is still trying to get him to change his mind, Henry who has a gammy leg. Then there's the sound of a fall. (1st C) Henry's fall has been broken by a ledge. He shouts to Martin for help, yelling that he's hurt his bad leg. Martin hesitates. He can either escape, or return down the escarpment and get help. In doing so, he will get himself into all sorts of further trouble. He sacrifices his final goal - escape and goes and gets help(2nd C) which leads to the resolution.

He's in loads of trouble, but has come good in the process, and he is given another chance, one that he takes. So, the theme has been addressed, his motivation to climb the escarpment is achieved, and in a sense he escapes his situation – by developing beyond the troubled boy. You can see that not only is his self-esteem on the way to being restored by behaving honourably but you can create in Martin an insight into his brother, who has been contacted after the break-out. Martin discovers that his brother has been desperately worried once informed of Martin's 'bunking off'. In a phone call (resolution) it is revealed that the bullying has been to try and toughen him up for when the brother is no longer around to care for him. He did indeed steal the trainers so that Martin wouldn't feel ashamed.

This is just an example and you could leave the resolution far more open ended with the contents of Martin's return phone call left to the reader's imagination, though there is an indication that there is a way forward.

Can you see how we've used the components, but taken a moment out of the flow of a life to explore the theme, rather than creating the flow of a life, as one would in a novel.

For your interest, you might have noticed that it contains the three unities, time, place and action.

Exercises

Read literary short stories, and those written with a market in mind, the genre short stories. See how they are moments taken out of the flow of a life, but with regard to the past and future.

Exercises:

Read other short stories, and ask the above questions of them.
Pick which short story you like best. Write two pages saying why.
Which do you like least? Say why.
Write a short story ending with. 'Well, he would, wouldn't he?'
Write a short story, starting with. It was too hot

General Exercises

Write about meeting a celebrity. Tell it twice. The first time from your point of view, and then from the celebrity's.

Forcing characters to confront fear is an effective way to generate conflict. But why should a character confront it, and not just deny the fear? Write about a fear confrontation.

Write about the most serious health or injury problem you've ever faced.

Write a page about someone with a hobby. What is it, and why do they do it, and what does it mean to them? What else is going on in their life?

If success was the only option, what would you do?

Ask questions of the world around you, and the people. Immerse yourself in the minutiae

Take a common cliché and write about it as though it was a literal truth. She went green with envy. He heart swelled with pride.

Chapter 6 The Sub-plot

We've dealt with a plot, and now we need to just take a look at a sub-plot.

Sub-plots are used within novels, rather than short stories. If you consider the length of a novel the linear plot can be relentless and narrow. Sub-plots can provide relief. It can just give pause, time out to reflect on what has so far been achieved within the novel. It can allow the reader to identify with another character, which will help inform them and explore the theme in more depth, though the main struggle will usually be the protagonist's.
Sub-plots are threads in a weave that attach to one or more secondary characters. So, to clarify the above:

You can think of sub-plots in two ways.

1. As brief enlighteners of a situation, in which the author changes point of view (more on this in the next chapter) to go into the body of another character in order to see the action or reaction from their perspective.

2. As a separate thread or plot, in which the other character (secondary and either mentor or antagonist) pursues a course which is relevant to the protagonist, but subservient.

Think back to Martin and the bus accident. If we created a brief enlightener of the situation we could switch to Henry's point of view as the bus goes over, to have his take on the situation. Then we go back to Martin, at the start of the next chapter. It's best not to diffuse the reader's identification by switching point of view back and forth between characters again and again within the same scene.
As a more substantial enlightener and separate thread we could go to No 2, and give alternate chapters to Henry as he remains injured in the damaged bus. Whilst Martin struggles to achieve his goal, matters in the bus can be reaching a critical point. Henry can be developing his character by standing up for Martin when the others have no faith in him. This can SHOW us Martin's life and problems without having to learn it from Martin. So whilst Henry is secondary to Martin, in his own sub-plot he is the protagonist.

As writers you would manage to sort out Henry's sub-plot by using the Zigzag Path in the same way as you would have done with Martin. But leave Henry's Zigzag Path until you've accessed Martin's story. Why? Because, and I know I'm banging on, the sub-plot is always subordinate to the main action but has to complement it. It will have its own rising arc, and resolution and character development, but these usually correspond to the main plot's shape and components, such as theme.

Similarly we could have a sub-plot in Audrey's story, headed by Stan. Then we would be privy to his actions and ill-doings. We would be served up his backstory along the way, as he and Audrey act and react to one another. In this way, tension would be served.

Bear in mind that novels are sometimes written today with equal plots for about 4 protagonists. This is fine, but to begin with I strongly advise that you stick to the one main plot. It's a lot to handle to do it any other way.

Exercise

1. Look at films, and read books and identify the sub-plots and their use in that scenario.

2. Create a sub-plot for Stan

3. Create a sub-plot for Henry

4. Write in Henry's point of view as the bus goes over. Then pick up the beginning of the next chapter in Martin's point of view as he lies in the road. What is he thinking, feeling, seeing, hearing, doing?

Chapter 7. Viewpoint or Point of View – they mean the same thing.

When writing fiction, we're striving to draw in the reader to the point where they identify primarily with the protagonist, and the journey he or she is undertaking.

For that reason, it is, in my opinion, best to choose a single viewpoint/point of view - in other words, to see the story through one person's eyes - within a scene, switching in an organised manner to another viewpoint and using a separate scene within the same chapter, as we have just discussed in the chapter on sub-plot. That scene might only be a paragraph in length, but it is still separate.

As a beginner writer I was in and out of every character in every scene which in retrospect weakened reader identification. With greater experience, I've chosen to stay with the main character in any given scene. If I break into multi viewpoint momentarily, it is usually for a reason but sometimes by mistake! Yes, we all make them, and the world doesn't stop, neither does the novel fail. But it's worth trying to strive for as much clarity and empathy as possible.

Why would I break into multi viewpoint? I might want the reader to see how the scene has been misunderstood by a secondary character, or to reveal their hidden reaction. But it could as well be done taking a separate but brief scene within the chapter, even if that scene is just a paragraph or two.

Let's just look at an example of point of view in use. I'm using a brief excerpt from a scene in Practising Wearing Purple, and during it we are in Barbs' point of view, in her sub-plot. Barbs had her sub-plot in her own chapters because she enlightened the theme in a profound way. I'll begin it with Kate talking to her. Yes, Kate is leading the discussion, but we are not IN her.

'Great,' Kate said, 'So you went to the hospital, had your consult, went shopping without waiting for the sales. When have you ever not waited for the sales? Then you rang me, picked me up, drove me here, not saying a word.'

I might not have had time to wait for the sales, Barbs wanted to say.

Here, we're being made aware of what is in Barbs head, so we're in her point of view, in her body receiving Kate's words. This is Barbs' scene, and our involvement and feelings are with her.

The next chapter is in Kate's point of view from Kate's position and we are in her head. As the protagonist she has the main plot line. Anything that happens with Barbs in these chapters will be seen and interpreted from Kate's perspective. I must say here, that many authors switch viewpoint about. I simply feel it is best not to, especially in the short story. You must decide for yourself. If you're having problems with viewpoint, try an exercise: Stay in the first person for a scene. As an example – be Kate. *I said to Barbs, ' So you went to the sales...'* Then change it to third person, still staying in Kate's point of view.

Let's look properly at 1st, 2nd and 3rd person at this point.

Viewpoint can also mean the 'person' in which the story is to be told. In other words, are you going to tell your story from the first or third person?

The First Person.

I settled back in the carriage, watching Esther laugh at Harry.

The advantages are that it's vivid and immediate. As a reader you are there. There's no confusion and it removes the barrier between the writer and reader. It is also virtually impossible, as I've just suggested, to slip viewpoint from one character to another and therefore weaken the tension and empathy. This though, is also its restriction.

It stops you from going into any other character's viewpoint, or sub-plot, should that be applicable. I have to say here that the first person, and third are increasingly being interwoven, with first person novels carrying sub-plots in the third person. It's a good idea to get used to writing in one or the other before you start experimenting. But do read some mixed novels, just to see what's happening out there.

The third person.

Hannah settled back in the carriage, watching Esther laugh at Harry.

It can be as vivid and immediate as the first person, as long as the writer stays in Hannah's viewpoint and only expresses everything from Hannah's perspective within a given scene. The third person also allows for a multiple viewpoint. At a later stage of the novel, Harry goes off to South Africa, so we can go with him, in his viewpoint and sub-plot

The second person.

You're sitting there, watching Esther laugh at Harry.

The second person is tricky, so be careful. It's almost as though the author is dictating how you will receive the novel and I think it's a hard 'person' to sustain. But that's just my opinion.

The omniscient viewpoint.

This is the God-eye viewpoint; that which observes and tells.

Who could have known, as Hannah settled herself in the carriage and watched Esther laugh at Harry that her heart was breaking…

It's not often used today, because it can be considered objective and distancing. It is certainly seldom used in a short story, though at times in a novel it can explain how your characters came to be as they are. Remember this can also be conveyed by showing, not telling.

Exercise

Find a scene in the novel you're reading. It will be written in one of the viewpoints we've discussed. Rewrite it in each of the other viewpoints. Then rewrite it in the original again, using one of your versions as the 'hard' copy. Then compare with the original. It will be in your voice. Do this with another two scenes, from another two novels or short stories.

Exercise

Read a short story, and a novel. Examine viewpoint, and see how it enhances the story to remain in one person's viewpoint in any given scene – or not. Or do you prefer it relentlessly multi-viewpoint? It's up to you.

Chapter 8. Flashback

Unlike real life a story doesn't have to take place chronologically. The author can move backwards and forwards through time, but why should they wish to do so?

No story can ever recount every little happening that influences the main character as he develops through life. Sooner or later, however, it may become necessary for something from the past to be explained in order to understand properly what is happening in the present. This can be conveyed by interior monologue, as we have already seen, dialogue, or by flashback, which is the creation of a retrospective scene.

A flashback is usually triggered by a present day image. It could be something like the smell of roasting coffee, the billowing of a white curtain, or as in the case of Audrey and the Leylandii story, the repetition of the sentence 'It's all a matter of timing.' To create a flashback the writer could go into the scene that featured the sister actually saying these words.

For that moment of flashback, the character is back in the past, feeling the sadness, passion, rage, and what's more, they take us, the reader, with them. Do read widely to see how others handle it, because it's important not to halt the pace of the story.

A flashback is a technical device that can be used to underline any situation, or give punch to any point you want to make. The mention of timing in Audrey's story is important. It's something we need to underline. It aids our understanding of the story. Don't be too obvious. This following example is how not to do it. *The smell of coffee reached her. She peered into the shop, thinking back to when she had been...*

Try just a bit harder, push yourself further - SHOW. *She stopped in the open doorway, hearing the coffee grinder, seeing the large Italian behind the counter reaching for a bag, then laughing up at his customer. It had not been an Italian behind the counter in Rosamund Street. It had been Arthur's mum, her hands gnarled, her mouth loose from too much booze, even as it had been on the day...*Then you can create a scene taking us back.

Exercise: Find examples of flashbacks in the novels you are reading. Note how it's done, and then write a flashback for either Martin or Audrey.

Chapter 9. Exposition. Dialogue, incorporating setting, action, pace and the use of language.

We have already talked about exposition, and you have worked on SHOW not TELL. You have created scenes that contain the necessary components of setting, dialogue, body language, symbolism. In other words you have already worked on how to bring your work to life. Crucial to this is finding your own voice, and you have already worked with exercises to help including the daily pages. Do remember the importance of destroying them.

In this chapter we'll be talking about dialogue, incorporating setting, action, pace and the use of language to help you improve on the work you've already undertaken.

Dialogue

Dialogue is one of the most important facets of creating believable characters but is considered by many new writers to be difficult.

It really isn't, if you've managed to get inside your character's skin, and understand them. I'm sure you did well in the breakwater scene, and I'm sure you've been observing many dialogues between those about you.

Let's just take a minute to look a little more carefully at the whole bundle of trouble.

We all talk, both inside our heads, and outside; by body language if not by speech.

Inside our head it's a thought process, which is called interior monologue. If words actually come out of our mouths it is almost invariably dialogue, rather than monologue. I say invariably, because I most certainly speak aloud to myself, if only to emphasise something in my head. Your character might well do that.

Yes, we talk a great deal. We talk to relate to others, and to pass on information. We also chatter about nothing. And often what we do talk about is shapeless and without depth. Why? Because chattering is vital for real-life communication. It's our way of reaching out, or so I tell my husband as he 'tunes out'!

Think how we bump into neighbours in the street.

'Hi, lovely day isn't it. Are you well? You look great. I'm just off to post a letter to Dink in Australia.'

'Oh, how is she? Are her legs better? Mrs Jones from Bridport has bad legs. Her mother had the same problem.'

'Really? Just goes to show… Well, look at that, haven't seen a gull so far inland before. Yes, goes to show just how much genes matter. People say sometimes leg things skip a generation.'

'Red hair is supposed to, isn't it?'

We stop and start, and interrupt and listen, and are appalled, bored, amused, and what's more, we love every moment of it, or at least I do. Dialogue is our lifeblood, gossip even more so. As writers, I give you total permission to earwig any gossip you please. Call it research.

But chatter doesn't necessarily progress our lives, as dialogue needs to progress a plot, theme and the whole caboodle.

So, in fiction we need to think of the purpose of the words that are going to pour forth! In fiction, if I had brought Dink into the conversation it would be to convey some important information. Dink would be relevant to the story, and its progression. In fiction I would not stop and start, and interrupt unless I was doing it quite deliberately. Dialogue is a device. All the components are there to be used by you to explore an idea.

Dialogue has specific functions:

1. To reveal and flesh out the character.
2. To move the plot forward and in so doing, crank up tension.
3. To convey information.
4. To break up chunks of narrative which are daunting on the page.
5. To invite empathy from your reader by translating some of the narrative into dialogue.
6. To improve the pace.
7. To convey mood.

These seven functions must be treated as a mantra. You must clutch them to you, sticky tape them on your forehead if necessary, so that you remember to consider your dialogue carefully.

Remember that though your characters must only speak when necessary, and for a reason, you must make it appear casual and natural. Dialogue must always fit the character's personality and mood.

Dialogue needs a sub-text to give it the depth that is often missing in mere chatter. Sub-text? Let's look at a woman who uses the word 'fun' too frequently.

'We hiked for 20 miles in the pouring rain. It was such fun.'

Often, this person initially appears spunky, but there can be a sub-text. The detail of it suggests that she is inviting sympathy. If she says *'We had a long hike, it was pretty wet, but I enjoyed it'* somehow that is more believable.

The detail of the first statement is revealing. 20 miles is a huge distance. *'It was fun'* sounds detached. It sounds as though she is **expected** to make light of anything related to her own discomfort. Perhaps it's what she **expects** of herself. Perhaps, minimising everything makes her life bearable. Perhaps she is with someone who bullies her. She needs help but can't ask for it.

Or/and it might be her way of securing her privacy. To admit explicitly that it wasn't to her liking invites questions, and a challenge. *'Well, why do it?'*

Whatever she really means, there **is** a sub-text there.

Remember to listen to the sub-text in your earwigging and conversations - it's there more often than we realise. And think back to Audrey and that important sentence uttered by her sister, about timing. The sub-text is clear. Remember to read features in the newspapers, which often discuss sub-text.

We've done a lot of work on SHOW not TELL already, and if you think back to the breakwater scene, I think you could manage to feed some sub-text into your conversation with the person who joins you at the breakwater. Especially if you have already done your Zigzag Path on the story line.

Let's talk a little bit more about ways in which you can convey feelings without 'telling'. You don't need me to tell you that we live in a visual age when information needs to be conveyed to the reader effortlessly. Seldom do readers have the time to wade through lengthy descriptions. Neither do they want to be fed the obvious, the **explicit** all the time. Try for the implicit; that which creates an image.

Explicit v implicit.

Explicit.
 'I ran out of petrol,' he said.
 'I don't believe you,' she replied.
Implicit
 'I ran out of petrol,' he said.
 'Oh?' she continued slicing the lemon.

Often what's left unsaid is more powerful than what's actually said, the implicit aids tension, that crucial ingredient which leads to the reader turning the page because it 'holds back' the punch line. What is this leading too? What is going to happen next?

With the explicit example, it was all over in a flash. We knew immediately that she didn't believe him, and therefore a chance to build more doubt, and consequently more tension, more character and empathy was gone. Whereas, with the implicit example, there is doubt. I want to know what happens next, how he tries to explain himself, and whether she really believes him or not. It can end with the explicit for dramatic affect.

Let's look at it a little more carefully.

She continued slicing the lemon is a signal that she's unmoved, or at least biding her time. Will she stop, or won't she stop and address the matter? And while we're about it, what's she going to do with the knife when she makes up her mind? The image of a knife is useful.

Dialogue doesn't come on its own, it is set in the scene and will probably include the senses. Dialogue will involve the past, present and probably future. It will include pace, all of which reinforce the SHOWING the scene.

Let's improve on the **implicit** two liner above by creating a setting incorporating action and resonance of the past by drawing in **symbolism**, in just a few words. Symbolism has a chapter of its own. This is a taster.

 'I ran out of petrol,' he said.
 'Oh?' she continued slicing the lemon. A pip caught on the blade. She shook it onto the pine chopping board, which had too many scars. Alex stared at them, her hand still. The board was as old and battered as her marriage. She turned, the knife still in her hand, the light catching the serrated blade.

So here I've set it very easily, and summed up the fact that though I haven't said this has happened before, it clearly has. The board is symbolic of her life. She's scarred. She turns, moving the plot forward. The knife is still in her hand. The tension is building. Is she going to ask for the receipt, kill him, or ask if he wants lemon in his gin? Who knows? As an exercise you can finish it if you like. But you can see that **you** could as easily have written this, because your unconscious would help you bring all these facets to your work. By now you would have BEEN her, in that moment, **showing** this scene.

Consider another longer scene. It is a version of one we've all seen many times on the television, or in a film, or read in a book.

'I'm sorry to have to ask you questions so soon after your loss, Mr Edwards.' (dialogue punctuation goes inside inverted commas*) DS Harris shifted in his chair. He hated this part of the job, hated choosing his words, watching to see if one would trigger a mine, when probably the poor sod was just what he seemed.* (So we know we're in Harris's viewpoint through the use of interior monologue, which also shows something of his nature, his job. We also realise there is a question mark over the loss experienced by Mr Edwards, some doubt/tension. We also know his name – it's now personalised.)

Edwards sat across the desk from him. 'You have your job to do.' His voice was quiet, almost limp, but how else would a father feel? For a moment DS Harris felt moved by pity, then experience re-asserted itself. (More interior monologue. Harris is arguing with himself about how a father would feel. He is **receiving** Edwards' behaviour, and is assuming things. He is clearly an experienced copper and though something bad has happened, he's trying not to feel pity – yet.) *He ran his finger round his collar. 'It's a bit hot, Sir. D'you mind?' He nodded to the window.* (So, now it's become clear that this is Edwards' office, since Harris is asking to have the window opened. We're being shown, not told. And that it's hot, and that he's in a 'proper' shirt. We already know he's not in uniform, because he's DS – Detective Sergeant.)

Edwards stared as though he did not understand, before lifting his hand in acknowledgement. (This makes it feel as though Edwards is beyond words. Whatever has happened is draining him. The action of the hands, both Harris's and Edwards help the pace along, and set the characters more firmly.)

Young DC Sally Taylor almost tiptoed across the busy carpet to the window. Harris watched her slip the catch. She moved well, too well and he'd have to keep reminding himself he was a happily married man if she stayed on his patch. She eased open the sash window, her linen jacket hitching up at the back. Along with the breeze came the sound of the fairground. (So, gradually we're building up the scene. No need to lay it all out in the first two lines. Let it grow. Now we have Sally Taylor, tiptoeing across a busy carpet. It's a shorthand description of Taylor's actions and appearance and the possibilities inherent in the 'working relationship'. It is not a blow by blow account of the woman herself or Harris's backstory. To keep it literally grounded I have integrated the busy carpet into the description.)

Harris hadn't realized it was so close, and now he shook his head at Taylor, who slammed it shut. (We now know that the fairground is important, without being told, and we have a horrible feeling that it's to do with the 'loss'. The window slamming down is explicit, a sound effect and dramatic. The more staccato rhythm sharpens the pace and rhythm. Just what's needed, when the rest had been implicit)

Edwards was staring at the paperknife he had snapped in two. (implicitly showing without explanation/telling what he was doing, but again the rhythm has sharpened up the pace)

'I'm surprised to see you at work today, Mr Edwards?' Harris kept his voice carefully neutral. (We still don't know what's happening, but the pace and rhythm, though still progressing the plot, has slowed again. This is not unlike a piece of music, is it? There is a huge sub-text building here and our interest is focussed on Harris and Edwards and the problem -(is he, or isn't he guilty) though it's Harris driving the scene, and it will be his struggle we follow, both professional and personal.

Consider the piece from Barbs and Kate again, and try to see the sub-text:

Kate, who has already been established as a nice but repressed woman with a domineering husband is worried about her mother-in-law. Barbs, the mother-in-law, has just been to the oncologist. It is an appointment Kate knew was in the offing. The two women are having coffee at a café by the beach.

'Great,' Kate said. 'So you went to the hospital, had your consult, went shopping without waiting for the sales. When have you ever not waited for the sales? Then you rang me, picked me up, drove me here, not saying a word.'

I might not have had time to wait for the sales, Barbs wanted to say.

Barbs has a sub-text which Kate is anxious to discover. Though not in Kate's viewpoint we are being shown Kate's anxiety. This anxiety is obvious from the rhythm of her language. She is listing things, having no time for trivia. At the same time we are being brought up to date on the sequence of events. We also gather that Barbs has broken a habit, that of always shopping in the sales. Why? The whole passage invites tension. Kate does not ask outright. Technically, it would lead to an answer too quickly, and also, Kate is scared of the answer.

This passage is not telling why Barbs is acting in this way, it is instead, inviting us to ask the question, enter into the tension. It is inviting our complicity. Rather than reply immediately, I rely on interior monologue, in other words, I go into the head of Barbs. She hints but still it is not revealed. The reader has to wait if they want to know more.

There are, however, always other ways of writing a passage. Nothing is ever the right one. I could have had some stops and starts to achieve the same effect, but they'd have been controlled stops and starts, always with a point in mind.

For instance, if I pick up where Kate says:

'Then you rang me, picked me...'
'I wanted to...' Barbs interrupted.
'Wanted to what?' Kate touched her hand.
'Never mind,' Barbs looked out to sea. Never mind. How could talking help?

This perhaps works better, here on these pages, but the other best suited the rhythm of the language of the novel. You just need to remember the balance of your work. You need the setting, the sub-text when necessary, the rhythm, the reason for the dialogue in the first place. Remember to use the senses.

Can you see the level at which one needs to write? It's not rocket science, it just needs empathy, planning and thinking about. You can do this easily, trust me.

To help you understand dialogue, you should read published work. When you read make sure you analyse. I cover this in more detail towards the end of the book, but note from the previous passages, how dialogue increases the pace, empathy, understanding and progresses everything. Be aware that if the writer doesn't use dialogue, but instead explains what is happening it will slow up the pace. It won't be vivid. It won't transport the reader into the scene. Dialogue is a crucial exposition tool.

A few other tips:

When writing dialogue, you must set aside perfection. Ignore our school grammar.

For instance, unless the character is pedantic, it would be unusual for them to say,

'I cannot carry this case on my own.'

Though use it by all means if the character is annoyed and stressing the point. I mean, haven't we all said that through gritted teeth when left to lug all the cases while someone else fiddles with that, oh so heavy, key.

Read dialogue aloud as you write. See how it sounds. Be aware of your rhythm. If dialogue is to convey distress, I suggest that the words will be simple, the sentences brief, or mere phrases. It will be as though the character is trying to breathe and grasp the reality of the situation. Act it out. My children have ceased to be alarmed at this deep voice issuing from the study as I become my male characters.

Remember that action reinforces the setting, the presence of the characters: *'Wanted to what?' Kate touched her hand.* Though don't over egg the pudding. Too much and it spoils. It comes down to balance again, and it takes a while to get that right. Don't worry, it will come.

Dialogue must be used gracefully and not sledge-hammered into place. You can omit speech modifiers if it is obvious who is speaking.

An example of a speech modifier. *'I told you not to come here,'* **John said, holding up his hand.**

Which could become. *'I told you not to come here.'* **John held up his hand.** Instantly the **pace** is increased, and the image is just as firm.

Beware of toad's spawn dialogue:

> *'I told you not to come here.'*
> *'I don't care what you said.'*
> *'Someone might have seen you.'*
> *'They didn't. I made sure.'*
> *'Oh yes, like the time before.'*

The complete absence of speech modifiers or setting makes it difficult to follow just who is saying what. It also makes it impossible to create a specific image, which denies the reader complicity. Use dialect sparingly. The odd regional phrase is sufficient.

Dialogue exercises

1. A man returns a wheelbarrow he borrowed ages ago from his neighbour, whose grass has run riot. Write explicit dialogue, with the interior monologue running under each line. In other words, write what they are **really** saying to one another using toad's spawn dialogue.
2. Take a piece of narrative from a novel and turn it into dialogue. You may use speech modifiers and setting.
4. Convey sympathy in a ten line section of dialogue including the following words. Line. Contact. Red. Cracked.
5. Convey regret in a ten line section of dialogue using the same words.
6. Convey anger in a ten line section of dialogue using the same words.

Chapter 10. Exposition. Show/Tell, including tension. Metaphor and simile. More explicit/implicit.

I think the 'show not tell' situation bears reinforcement. As I said, when discussing speech tags, toad's spawn dialogue makes it difficult to picture the scene, to create an image.

Concentrate on those words, 'picture' and 'image'. As I've said, we live in a visual age, in which time is of the essence, and people are used to receiving information from the screen almost without realizing, and very quickly.

The screen is a medium where no black words on white paper come between the viewer and the action to distract them. Like it or not, as writers, your words must be as invisible as possible. You must tuck that ego away, and strive to bring texture, a sense of place, a sense of the characters, the warmth of the sun, the smell of coffee, the sound of the wind, the taste of fear wham, bam, straight to that 'receiver' in your reader. You need to aid the reader's imagination, and show them everything.

We've already worked on creating scenes, but let's do just a bit more, just as you would if you were on a writing course, one that builds your skills week after week. We've already accepted that believable characters must do believable things, in a believable place. We need to create an illusion of reality, by creating images using as few words as possible. Yes, yes, I know we are capable of the most glorious prose, but it slows things up, it intrudes.

Let's take the opening of a short story or novel. Gone are the days of long rambling introductions and descriptions of characters and their past and present, the setting and period. Today it's straight into the story, much as it was in the breakwater scene. We're straight in the normal world but at a point of change. It is from this point of change that the journey will begin.

Let's take a look at pace. We saw it in action in the chapter on dialogue. Rhythm of language can alter pace, but let's look at its place as part of the choreography of the scene.

We must not slow the pace, or bore our readers before they've even reached the end of the first page, but we must also allow pauses to be part of the fabric of our work. We must raise tension, then let it slump, or pause, for just a moment. We then let it build again. Remember the jagged line in the diagram.

Let's look at the beginning of the film, The Bodyguard.

In the opening scene there are three shots, the lovely Kevin Costner is crouching with a gun, protecting his client. This shows us his normal world, the one from which he is, unknown to himself, about to leave if the point of change rule is applied. We see he's a professional, a cool dude, a good shot. No-one is telling us. No-one is sitting in an armchair saying to dear old Whitney Houston that Kevin is the man to have as bodyguard because of this and that reason.

We are being **shown**.

But that's not all. The pace is already moving on - courtesy of tension. Are there any more assailants? Here we have a tension hook. What is the answer, does he get out of it? Of course he does. Challenge No 1 one faced and overcome. He has a meeting with his boss, who is grateful - a moment of pause. He returns to his own home - a moment of pause. Then Whitney's aide arrives. We're off again. There's your pace.

Tension hooks:

Tension hooks are essential. You need questions raised within chapters, and scenes, and pages, and paragraphs. You need them raised at the end of a chapter, to make the reader unable to put the book down, to make them want to read on. Remember the implicit example of dialogue. Remember Martin climbing the escarpment. Maybe his hand slips, will he be able to recover? Perhaps in another scenario someone didn't quite hear, and the question has to be repeated, or the door sticks as someone tries to open it. All sorts of little things can be written in with subtlety, and the reader isn't aware that they are tension hooks, but they are. You will need another bigger one at the end of the chapter. Perhaps we meet the bully for the first time, but we don't know if he's friend or foe.

Perhaps the protagonist is stuck in a lift. Leave it there, and deal with the solution in the next chapter.

Now I'm going to take you over yet again, the implicit just to make sure you understand its importance, and how easy it is.

Consider this example of explicit and implicit description:

a)   *The man was fat.*

This is explicit. It's often our first draft of the image. It's the synopsis thought, the report, the easy way out for the writer. We are only dealing with one layer of information here, but could create a better illusion of reality, and draw the protagonist into the scene, so that we see it from their point of view. Try this.

b)   *The man's shirt stretched across his belly. She could see the folds of his stomach.* This is implicit. There is a picture here, an image, and I'm waiting for her to say or think something else. There's tension.

Consider this:

She stood in the kitchen doorway. There was tomato sauce splashed on the table, and a cigarette stubbed out in the half eaten fried egg sandwich.

In real life we take in a view quickly. What we are being shown here are shorthand details that log into our brain's database and register, without the writer's words coming between us and our involvement. But more than that, it raises questions. Why was the sandwich only half eaten? Did the person leave in a hurry? Details are important, they leave a question in our minds, if that is indeed the writer's intention, and what's more, we are in collusion with the protagonist in the scene. We are in their body.

If we were being told it would have been written:

She stood in the kitchen doorway, **and saw a mess**. The writer could go on to say: *There was tomato sauce all over the table, and a cigarette stubbed out in the half-eaten egg sandwich.*

Just a small change, but the writer could have trusted the reader to grasp the point. But I don't think I'd bother with the narrator's voice explaining it as well as us 'seeing' it. We want to be in there with the character.

Exercise

Locate the normal world, and the point of change, and the first hook, and the first pause in two films, or plays that you should go and see and a story.

Exercise

You are a boss, about to sack a worker. The worker's response to this is alarming.
Write the normal world of the boss. The first tension hook, the point of change, a pause, the second tension hook. Write it Show not Tell.

Let's do further work on how to evoke the impression you want to create.
What is it we want to create? A sense of place, a sense of 'being there', something vivid and immediate.
Let's pull together setting, action, pace, rhythm, the past and present, senses and mannerisms to create an example image.
*Thomas checked his gun, radio and knife .(*A list of actions. Fast pace/rhythm.*) It was the usual procedure (*So he's done this before*) He sat back on his haunches. (*Slower pace/rhythm – pause*) Around him the radios crackled, the hanger lights were dim and the troops mere shadows.(*List of setting and action - pace up again*) He chewed his thumb nail. (*Pause – focus back on him, mannerism showing he's nervous).

The use of metaphor to evoke images. A metaphor is a figure of speech in which one thing is identified with another.

The remnants of love had just walked out of the door. As far as she was concerned, Phil was an empty can of soup, all debris and nasty smells.

Thomas's scene fragment does not contain metaphor, but is revealing none the less. Let's look at the use of metaphor, simile and precise image as a brief introduction to Chapter 11 which explores symbolism.
Phil was an empty can of soup tells us something of Phil as she perceives him. What does it also tell us about her? Firstly, she is the main character in this sketch. We know this because it is through her eyes that we are seeing this scene - it is from her point of view, or her viewpoint. (Whichever way you want to put it) We are left to wonder - will he, won't he walk back in

again? What has happened? Why? When? Where? What? Who? How? Back to Phil. It seems a harsh metaphor. Is the main character a bitch, or has Phil done something pretty dire? I think I'd want to read on in order to know. The pace is snappy, the metaphor is used in context, and the whole paragraph is absorbed as a scene.

The metaphor works well because something ordinary has been used in an extraordinary way. Basically, the brain's database is easily accessed by this familiar precise image which will trick the reader's mind into short cutting to a 'state of affairs'.

I could have used simile rather than metaphor. **Simile** likens one thing to another. It uses the word like or as. **Metaphor** is a condensed simile without the word like/as. Both create an instant and powerful image, one that goes beyond the conventional, but uses the conventional.

My life is a toilet bowl. (**A metaphor**) and said to be used by Billie Holliday.

My life is like a toilet bowl. (**A simile**)

I consider the metaphor above to be stronger than the simile, but it depends on the text as to which one would use.

Phil is an empty can of soup. It is stronger than - *Phil is like an empty can of soup.*

Use metaphor and simile sparingly though. They can be pretentious, and therefore too intense. Worse, if used unnecessarily it is visible use of language, and will distract the reader from the story.

Precise image or detail

Let's take another look at precise image or detail. There's a difference between a Cartier and Timex watch. Red equates with sexy. Look at the advertisements on the television, or in magazines. Without realising it, we are receiving symbols every day of our lives, which trigger an image in our subconscious. Red is used when the manufacturer wants to convey warmth, vibrancy, romance, sexiness, even danger. Red roses. Red sunsets. Red cars Something explosive or dangerous. A red traffic light warns of danger if we don't stop.

A girl in a red dress tells us one thing and a girl in wearing a pastel floating dress tells us something else. We would expect her nature to be soft and gentle. If this turns out not be be so, then that it an added tension twist. But the initial image would inform that scene in a shorthand way.

If someone carries a bowl of eggs our subconscious would probably equate it with birth, rebirth, fertility. If one of the eggs is broken, it could signal the fracture of the cycle of life, or a relationship, or a death.

All this is subliminal. We don't consciously realise the message we are receiving. If one character breaks another's most precious possession, it means more than just the destruction of an object. It is often a sub-text for something much deeper, a destruction of that relationship or breaking away from the past.

Exercises

1. Show a room which is set up for a children's party. No guest has yet arrived. Show the room when the last guest has left – use your senses, and one metaphor and one simile, and be brief. Try for a few potent images that will short cut to the reader's imagination.

2. Show a meeting between a mother-in-law and her son-in-law. In the first BE the mother in law. In other words, she is the main character in the scene. It is from her point of view. Now BE the son-in-law. It is his point of view, it is his scene.

Chapter 11. Exposition. Symbolism

What is symbolism? It can be considered the use of a visual metaphor to underline a theme.

We have just seen that metaphor is a figure of speech in which one thing is identified with another. 1) He is a tiger when roused. My life is a toilet bowl. It doesn't mean that they have been transmogrified into the item. The item is being used to symbolise something.

Think of a woman stuck fast on a water slide, much as her life is stuck. How is she to move on?

Let's use a cliché to make things clear. Think of a butterfly trapped in an attic, beating at the window. A woman's there, sorting out stuff. She uses every means in her power to open the window, and release the butterfly. Its freedom means something more than the mere fact that the butterfly has escaped. It means that the butterfly is a symbol of her own need to escape.

Symbolism is a natural aspect of communication as we touched on briefly in the previous chapter. We'll look at it more closely now. Symbolism is with us from our earliest days. We used symbols at play – making items stand for various aspects of our games. Fingers pointed become guns. This pretend action is often carried on into adulthood, to symbolise, amusingly or otherwise, someone's attitude to another person, or a reaction to some point they make. When we see it in films we immediately understand it, it's in our cultural past.

Advertisers strive to connect their products to our cultural understanding. To abstract notions like success, nostalgia, or domestic bliss. Think of the ads on TV which show a cleaner which whizzes through the work, and leaves us FREE as we once were – and could be again. Certain brands of coffee become synonymous with romance as we once knew it, or would like to know it, and bread with the way things were, whizzing downhill on a bike. We understand more than the actual scene appears to be saying because it is working on several levels, as we have been doing.

Think again of colours. Colours through association have become a sign or a symbol. In chocolate for instance, black may symbolise daring and mystery.

If you think of white shoes for men – a survey showed that following a series of early films that look has become synonymous with con men. (What about the character in Dad's Army, who wore whiteish shoes)

But what has symbolism to do with writing?

Everything. I've just said that it is a natural aspect of communication. Fiction is a representation of life, and symbols are central to all known human cultures. Symbolism enhances SHOW not TELL. Symbolism ensures that the message of the story is visible, without the need for TELLING, or commentary.

A symbol is a coded message and in many cases it is our unconscious brain which deciphers it. We need to know, as writers, how to use these messages, to add yet another layer of resonance to our work, to short cut to that part of our reader's brain that recognises such codes.

Let's look again at the butterfly.

A butterfly is considered by some to be ephemeral, fragile, perhaps helpless, at the mercy of greater forces. The release of that butterfly can have resonance for the character as we've just seen, one that strikes a chord with the reader. A) Perhaps release is what the protagonist wishes for herself. B) Perhaps it creates an image of something that happened long ago, in her past. C) Perhaps she is remembering a scene from her childhood, when butterflies were integral to a remembered image, one that involves a character she cared about, who then disappeared. **The writer decides the use of the metaphor but with the reader in mind. It can be one that recurs, especially in a novel. It can change its code. From being an object of fear it can become an object of triumph.**

Let's stay with the butterfly for a little longer and assume that the writer has used the butterfly in the attic as a symbol of restriction and helplessness, hence the protagonist's frantic need to release it. As the story progresses, and the character develops, the image of the released butterfly can become an integral motivator to release herself from her own predicament. She can then look at butterflies again in a less panic stricken way, once she has achieved her aim, and the theme is addressed (helplessness).

Story telling and poetry draw on cultural symbols to add depth and impact all the time. I read a short story about a pearl necklace which broke, and the pearls scattered to all four corners of the room. The way in which the story had been written indicated that the broken necklace was a symbol of loss, of an ending, (pearls are a symbol of tears – of either sorrow or joy). They are also reminiscent of an egg, which is a symbol of birth as I've already said. Let me repeat also that of you have an accidental breakage of an egg, it can be used as a code for death, for the end of life, or just the end – therefore there could also be a beginning. To go back to the pearls - the recovery of the pearls, the potential restringing of them, perhaps in a different way, or even their dispersal as earrings or whatever, was symbolic of...? You decide.

Incidentally, pearls are also symbolic of patience, purity and peace. So all of these log into our unconscious, and it is the way in which we, as writers, use the code that adds that resonance.

Symbolism needs a light hand. Its aim is to allow implication to resonate through detail, not as an example of our 'cleverness'. Beware the ego in writing.

To help yourself, take a look at any magazine and television ads. Red is sexy. If you have a bevy of red cars on a shimmering satin dais, then what is this, but the epitome of 'come on'. In other words, if you buy this car, you can't fail to pull. Red is warm, vibrant, exciting. It is also cruel, bloody. Use it as you will. Your reader will understand and decipher the code.   Also be aware that colours can find their way into our unconscious even if they are of eyes, and hair. Blue and grey are considered cool. Brown is warm. So maybe a detective should have blue eyes, or a certain type of detective.

You can use symbolism to evoke practically anything. A sunset which starts scarlet, and evolves to dramatic heights with gold flaring, with clouds racing, until the darkness of night sweeps it from the sky, could mean anything from the height and post height of passion, to something else you wanted to infer, and your reader would decipher the code within the context of your scene.

Track it in the work you read. Yet again, I say, readers today expect something easily accessible. It's a visual world, one in which they are bombarded with subliminal messages by virtue of advertisers, and writers who have hooked into this use of code. Readers will not mark time whilst you take up valuable space TELLING them cumbersome details because their minds are well versed in deciphering coded messages, and your mind is well versed in delivering the codes, if you remind yourself of the facts.

Exercises – Incorporate some symbolism.

1. Put yourself in a huge lofty ultra modern office. You are a woman in heels. (even if in reality you're a bloke) You've just entered. You click clack across the cool marble floor. To minimise the noise you try walking on your toes but you can see from the mirrors all around that you look ridiculous, diminished somehow. You give up, and return to the click clack. There's no other sound. The walls are white, the coffee table is glass. It's cool. The pictures are white and black abstract. Mr Soames is sitting at his desk, watching. So, as a writer you've already symbolised the man by his surroundings. Cool hard floor. Cool hard silent man. She's not silent. She's exposing herself to him with the noise she's making, much as prey does to a lion. It's chilling. BE there, create that scene.

Now, turn Mr Soames into a chaotic and warm person with suitable surroundings. Then create a stressed person. An old person. Someone heartbroken. Someone under investigation. In all of these, you would have to change not only the room, but the people and their body language.

1. Rewrite a passage from a newspaper, something you find interesting. Transform it into fiction, keeping up the pace, the tension, and creating a believable main character.

2. Cut a piece of paper into twelve squares. On six pieces write a noun. For instance: Table, tree, bike, sky, music, clouds. On the other six write a verb. For instance: Chop, drill, paint, lift, draw, carve. (To get these I thought of a job – building). Put them face down in two separate piles, take one from each and produce a creative sentence. Do this for all the words.

3. Turn the following paragraph into a scene.
Margaret was an interfering nuisance, always poking her nose into other people's business. The highlight of her day was a phone call to her mother, whose new husband she disliked.

Chapter 12. Editing. Research. Analysis. Synopsis. Conclusion.

We're going to close this handbook with brief notes on editing your work, research, analysis and synopsis.

Editing your work.

Leave your novel, short story or exercise for at least a week. When you return to it, you're more likely to be able to see the wood in spite of the trees. Read it. Above all, listen to your instincts. Something might not seem quite right. Reword it, or cut it.

If you have a writing circle, read it to the circle, be prepared to listen to their comments but ultimately trust your own judgement.

Have you adhered to the shape? Have you included all the components? Have you cluttered up the story with unnecessary detail, or just enough? Is your point of view as you intended? Do your characters come out and grab you by the neck and haul you into their world?

Have you created living breathing scenes that SHOW rather than TELL and are full of empathy? Have you included symbolism?

Guard against too much fancy literary footwork. Can you see your language intruding between you and the story? Have you used several words where one would do? A pet hate of mine is: She held the glass in her hand. Well, I would hope so, or is does she usually pick it up with her foot! Oh acid tongued woman - but you take my point.

When I wrote my first novel I thought all the time that there were not enough words for me to use. I felt I kept repeating myself. Well, you'll repeat yourself, but at the same time try for the specific modifiers like scalding instead of very hot. Check that your work is not cluttered by any unnecessary adverbs or adjectives. Go that extra yard and find a suitable noun or verb instead. As an exercise, you could try writing half a page of a scene, and allow yourself only one adverb and one adjective.

Is everything strictly relevant? Check that you haven't lost sight of the main character's journey and toddled off down a track, slowing the pace and losing reader identification and empathy?

The protagonist. Does he/she act in character throughout? Are they and their actions plausible? Have you reminded the reader of your characters' appearance from time to time? If it's a novel have you checked that they have aged correctly? Have they retained the same colour eyes? In one of mine because of a re-edit that went wonky this classic mistake occurred. S-o-o embarrassing. Does the protagonist keep an eye on the motivational ball? Is the theme resolved satisfactorily? Are there any loose ends; any characters abandoned, any threads flying about in the wind? Do you care about the characters? Is your empathy weak anywhere or rushed.

Try and ensure that you've balanced the implicit with the explicit.

Have you any toad's spawn dialogue?

Are your settings relevant? A trip on the river must be a device. The event must be there for a reason.

Can you see, feel, smell and taste your scenes?

Have you 'held back' or instead, rushed and missed an opportunity to create tension?

We've discussed flashback and its uses. Make sure that you have not over-used the device, and that, when you have incorporated it, it is gracefully done. Make sure that it has not stopped the pace. Ask yourself if it would it be better to deal with the issue chronologically.

Then pop it in a drawer for another week at least, a month preferably, before repeating the process. Yes, really. Tough at the coal face, isn't it.

Presentation of manuscripts.

If you're thinking of trying for publication at some stage remember wide margins, double-spacing, use one side of A4 only. Always send a SAE with your submission to a publisher or agent. If it's a short story send the whole story, having studied your market carefully first. Put FBSR on the front page. (First British Serial Rights) then you can use it again. If it's a novel, send a synopsis and three chapters with a brief letter, stating type of novel, length, and possible marketing angles. Are you a film star for instance?

Again, you need to study your market. Note the name of the publisher of books similar to yours, and send it to them. Alternatively, look in the annual Writers and Artists Year Book and see which agents handle your sort of work, or enter competitions. If you are placed it will enhance your CV and you must mention it in your brief letter, also mention any other publishing successes. You are trying to make yourself visible to the publisher.

Agents are wonderful, but just as overloaded as publishers. Many have lists that are full, but there are openings. Send to them, as you would a publisher, with the relevant information in your brief letter. All those now published once set out on this same trail, remember, and we made it. It often comes down to being in the right place at the right time, and rejection is sometimes not a reflection on your writing ability.

Subscribe to one of the writing magazines or access one of the internet writing magazines. They are full of useful information and markets.

Some writers say that beginner writers should consider the market and write to that end. I think beginner writers should enjoy their apprenticeship and write from the heart. It takes time to get it right, time to handle the techniques so that your voice comes through loud and clear.

Synopsis. (Unnecessary for a short story)

Initial letter

The initial letter should be brief, stating the type of novel or short story, the length, and any previous publication success. Please don't be too cocky, apologetic or long winded. Just keep it brief and clear. This is a reflection of you as a person, and your work.

The synopsis.

Again this should be brief, and between 2 and 10 pages, single spaced. There are several books devoted to the synopsis, and these are worth reading. The following notes are just a rapid breakdown.

Synopsis. This should be in present tense.

1. Explain the novel very briefly making sure you plug the title, state where it's set, and when, include the time span of the novel, and the length. Convey mood and tone of story. Funny, emotional etc.
2. Next section. Explain the protagonist. Give the name, age and social group. Give a cameo of the character, their motivation, backstory, and the theme and their development internally and externally.
3. Do this for the secondary characters, giving also their relationship to the protagonist, and their mentor/antagonist roles.
4. Show the main conflict in the plot. e.g. Step-family trying to stop Cinderella achieve her aim and why.
5. Show the shape briefly: Normal world. Point of change. 3 Cs. Resolution.
6. Show the key scenes in slightly more detail. (You could use an example of your exposition within the scene to support your expertise.)
a. The point of change.
b. The crisis/climax/crisis scenes.
c. The confirmatory scene, if there is one.

Include first three chapters to exhibit your talent.

You could add a brief biography of yourself to show who you are and any success you've had, and any angles which might help promote you.

Analysis of fiction

A writer cannot write without reading. Neither, of course can he write, without writing, writing, writing. But at some stage form must be addressed.

Study the sort of book or short story you'd like to write. For the purposes of this book, if you are interested in short stories, you will need to adapt the following analysis to suit a short story. In other words, where I say chapter, think of paragraph.

In general:

In each chapter observe how the story is being built up. Make notes on each chapter detailing the actions of the main characters. Observe the shape of each chapter. Ask yourself how tension is built up. Note the opening scene. The first chapter should be in the normal world at a point of change – is it? What is the theme? Is there a hint? In particular: Characters: Does the writer switch viewpoint to another character in a period of particular interest? Does it work? Is it clear? Would it be improved by staying in one viewpoint?

How does the writer show the effects of the actions of the protagonist/main character on others?

Do you feel the writer has 'become' his/her characters. Are you drawn in? Are you complicit? Do you care?

List the characters, their strengths and weaknesses and any quirks of personality. Note how one may be a foil for another. Note how the good are portrayed, and then the bad.

How do the characters interact with each other?

What is the back story? In other words, what caused the feuding, hate, romance, friendship and conflict?

Look for ways in which a character's actions help to build up the exposition.

Note the way a character is introduced both by physical description and personality.

Is the exposition implicit or explicit? Could it be improved? What do you feel overall about the nature of the exposition?

Is the picture built in a subtle way, or are you aware of intrusion? Do the words come between you and the action? Can you see the brush between you and the picture?

Note if there is an unusual or telling piece of description and personality.

Does it work? Does it improve the chapter and your perception of the character? Are all the senses brought into play?

Having analysed the characters, start to break down the chapters and each scene within them in detail.

How?

Narrative.

Write a précis of each scene. Just a couple of sentences describing the main dramatic point or how a character was motivated to act as they did.

Note the hook which hints at dramatic events still to unfold. The hooks keep the reader wanting to know what comes next and therefore turning the pages. Note how each setting is made visual to the reader, and calls on their other senses.

Note the description of the setting itself and how the characters acted out the drama in that setting. Was the setting made part of the scene, or was it told in a great slab of description? Is there a sense of place? Can you almost be in that place, see, hear, feel, smell what it is like?

What is the element of conflict building in every scene? How does it propel the plot forward? Every scene should reveal something about a character or advance the plot. Does it? Be aware of the way dialogue is used to reveal character and to forward plot.

Show don't tell.

See how a scene is acted out by the characters. Is the sense of place maintained? How do their actions convey their setting, their state of mind? How does the rhythm of their dialogue and the author's style, language and pace enhance the mood of the scene? Is there the use of implicit and explicit? Any symbolism? Any evidence of 'holding back'?

It is imperative that you engage the reader, and that they, as well as you, can empathise and identify with all the characters and their situation. Is there anyone who is not well imagined? If so, why? Is every character understandable? They may not all be likable, but they must be understandable in order to be realistic. If not, why not? Work it out.

See how thoughts and flashbacks are used. Are they an integral part of the scene, or do they disrupt the picture? Do they sit dead in the water, and remind you that you are a reader on the outside of the action?

Analyse each scene for its pace, and its peaks and troughs.

But for goodness sake, don't make your life a misery or worry about this if it seems too much. Just relax and if you prefer, simply notice in a laid back way what is really going on in every book, story, film and play you experience. Whether you unpick the threads with a fine tooth comb or merely take note as you involve yourself in fiction of all kinds, you will find that you the more you write, the more you see in the work of others.

*   *   *

And now we are at the end of our journey. I hope that you have enjoyed the experience, and have extended your writing ability through ***The Writer's Springboard.***

Can I give you any other words of advice? Let's see. I think you should consider attending writing groups, in the flesh or on line. I think you should sign up for writing courses and conferences such as Arvon, Ty Newydd, Swanwick and Winchester Writers Conference at which professional authors teach. I think you will gain from the tuition, and company and experience of others. The wisdom and enthusiasm of other writers helps to keep your own fire burning.

Remember to keep up the daily pages and observations. Remember to write from the heart. Life's too short to do anything else. You will find that giving shape to human problems and experiences in your creative writing can help you in your own life.

You're at the start of a wonderful change in your life, the start of a great affair between you and your creative imagination.

Remember that there is no need for medals, stars, prizes, publication to validate you. It is enough that you bring joy to yourself, satisfaction to yourself. It is enough to discover, and be the real you.

I cannot guarantee publication. I can only guarantee that you will find writing an empowering experience, and I wish you well, on the continuance of your journey of exploration.

Other books in the series

Writing Awake the Dreamweaver – designed to release creativity, reclaim your unique voice, and reveal the communicator within.

Bestselling author, Margaret Graham can be contacted about creative writing workshops, her own and at conferences, and her mentor service at:

www.margaret-graham.com and www.thewordforce.com

She is co-administrator of the Yeovil Literary Prize, the Yeovil Stage Play Prize and details of these creative writing competitions can be found on www.yeovilprize.co.uk